LEAN ENTERPRISE LEADER

HOW TO GET THINGS DONE
WITHOUT DOING IT ALL YOURSELF

LEAN ENTERPRISE LEADER
HOW TO GET THINGS DONE
WITHOUT DOING IT ALL YOURSELF

BY

STEPHEN HAWLEY MARTIN

RICHMOND, VIRGINIA

First Edition

ISBN 1-892538-47-4

If your bookseller does not have this book in stock,
it can be ordered directly from the publisher.
Contact us for information about discounts
on quantity purchases.

The Oaklea Press
6912 Three Chopt Road, Suite B
Richmond, Virginia 23226

Voice: 1-800-295-4066
Facsimile: 1-804-281-5686
Email: Info@OakleaPress.com

This book can be purchased online at
http://www.LeanTransformation.com

Contents

Introduction

Perhaps your company has taken steps toward becoming a lean enterprise, and things are going okay, but you've picked up this book because there's always room for improvement. Progress may have been made in manufacturing and downsizing may have taken place in other areas of the business, eliminating layers of supervisors. One problem may be those who remain find themselves struggling to keep their heads above water. It may seem they, and you, are expected to do more with less.

Maybe this is not the case at all. Perhaps manufacturing has been converted to lean but the rest of the organization is still operating the old, mass-manufacturing, bureaucratic way. Barriers between departments remain high. A siege mentality may have taken hold as department heads wait for the second shoe to drop. From your vantage point, things haven't changed much, except some people are working harder, and others appear to be little more than passengers on the bus. The championship mentality and esprit de corps you've read about in other lean operations does not exist.

A third possibility is that you are a leader in a service business who would like to apply lean principles. You know your company could provide customers with better service with less staff and overhead if everyone would work together with a sense of urgency and accountability. This would make the business more profitable and lead to happier customers, growth, success, and opportunities for everyone. But most around you are going through the motions, and a few individuals here and there do the heavy lifting, you included. There must be a way to motivate everyone so they all participate equally.

Whichever scenario describes your situation, this book's for you.

A few years ago I helped develop and edit a book called *Lean Transformation: How to Change Your Business into a Lean Enterprise*. This has proven to be the tool of choice for many to use to convert manufacturing operations into lean producers. It's become so popular it has sold more than 50,000 copies and been translated into half a dozen languages. *Lean Transformation* explains the "how to" of continuous flow, pull scheduling, inventory reduction and the building in of quality. It may be the best book of its kind. But it places the focus on manufacturing operations and does not go into great detail about how to get the bloat out of the rest of the organization, including how to break down the barriers between departments, disperse fiefdoms, and turn the entire operation into a well-oiled machine where everyone, regardless of his or her position, is pulling his or her own weight. The intent of this book is to explain how a company can reach this level of excellence.

Almost every organization has a few hard working individuals who make things go. The problem is the 90 percent who are not quite so conscientious or competent. This recalls to mind the saying, "Work flows toward competency unless abated," and the corollary, "If you want a job done, give it to a busy man [or woman]." Without a system in place to insure everyone pulls his or her own weight, a few individuals within an organization will end up doing all the work.

But this doesn't have to be.

You probably know several people in your organization you can count on to follow through on an assignment. You know others you cannot count on. Ask yourself, do you tend to call again and again on those you know will get the job done? Do you yourself sometimes take on more than you can handle because you have no one available you can count on? Do you sometimes put off a job that needs doing because you and those you can count are too busy? Yet, are there others you could assign if only you were confident they would follow through?

If you answer "Yes," you are managing by personality. This way of operating isn't fair to those who end up overloaded and overworked, yourself included—especially because there is a better way. This leadership system anyone can use regardless of their leadership skills will be explained. It will allow you and others to spread out the work, create a sense of urgency and accountability among the entire staff, and get everyone pulling their own weight and moving ahead toward clearly defined objectives.

Most top executives today know they could operate more efficiently if people would only come together and put forth a little more effort. Payroll costs would drop and company performance would improve because it would be possible to move faster to take advantages of opportunities in the marketplace. People closest to problems would make decisions and take the right actions to solve issues when they arise. But today an entrenched bureaucracy is holding them back. Decisions become mired in red tape. The head of this department and of that department do not see eye to eye, causing a time-consuming standoff. If only barriers could be eliminated. If only cross-functional teams would really operate as teams rather than forums for grievances.

It's not difficult to envision how things could be and ought to be. The hard part is seeing the way to move from where you are to where you'd like to be. How do you create a championship environment where everyone is working together toward a common goal instead of looking out for number one?

Read on. This book will tell you.

Chapter One: The Way Things Don't Have to Be

What I will describe here is true of many offices and factories. First, are the managers. They come in all shapes and sizes, each with his or her notion, perhaps misguided, of what it means to manage people. Some are like the overbearing teacher you had in third grade who believed she had to control everything. The managers in this category are assertive, aggressive, even intimidating. If you could peek inside them, you'd find they actually are scared to death and stressed almost to the breaking point they might overlook something. Heaven forbid they should ever make a mistake. And if they did, they'd never admit it to anyone, perhaps not even to themselves. Any lapse in judgment will go with them to the grave.

Some percentage of them believe they shouldn't waste time talking to employees, except when giving instructions. Fraternizing with with the working class could harm their image. Associating with employees in anything other than a "managerial capacity" could hurt them when promotion time comes, so they stick close to like-minded managers, and distance themselves from everyone else.

These managers are likely to be focused intently on making their production numbers because they think in terms of quarterly results, rather than long-term. They believe themselves responsible for virtually everything, which makes them very reactive. They often run around in a frenzy, putting out fires, and have a hard time finding a moment to sit down and think. As a result, they are almost never proactive and seldom think beyond the end of today's quitting time.

Nevertheless, all the frenetic motion they generate does have its rewards. Most companies that have a high percentage of managers operating this way treat them like aristocracy. They comprise an elite ruling class and are the only ones given supposedly "confidential" numbers about the company's overall performance. They go to seminars and receive training in a wide variety of skills beyond their immediate job, such as negotiating and hiring practices. And for the stress they endure, they receive handsome salaries and bonuses, comfortable offices, designated parking places, and company cars—to name just a few of the perks they typically enjoy.

Then there are employees. On the other side of a huge chasm, these folks generally are regarded by the managers, perhaps unconsciously, as unfeeling and unthinking robots. They typically do one particular job, and only that job, all day long, and aren't taught any skills beyond those needed for that job. Of course, they're not given any information about how the company is doing in general and have no responsibility or accountability for anything beyond their assigned task. Even this is limited because a separate quality inspection department checks what they produce. So, in reality, these employee robots are not even responsible for their own work. Naturally, they are extremely frustrated. Their spirit of innovation and risk-taking was killed off long ago.

New employees often arrive brimming with possibilities, enthusiastic at the opportunity to help out the company and to be of value. They offer suggestions with the best of intentions, but it doesn't take long for them to learn they're wasting their time. The suggestions they make are either ignored by supervisors, or they are told these suggestions will be taken under advisement. Nothing ever is done, of course, which is why employee robots no longer comment on all the things they see around them that could be improved. They've attended so many productivity circles and been subject to many supposedly miraculous "programs of the month" which have fizzled out that they have resigned themselves to the belief that corporate America will never do anything but abuse them.

Their thought process goes something like this: "This is where I work, but this is not where I really want to be. The reason I'm here boils down to one thing and it's called 'money.' I put in my eight hours and I go home. Why should I do more? They don't want my ideas." The result is most employees work within their little self-defined squares and do exactly as they are told, but no more, and maybe even less if they can get away with it.

THE POINT I've tried to make is there are two classes of people in most companies—workers and executives—and this sets up a counterproductive "us against them" mentality. Many outward signs call attention to which side a person is on, reinforcing the division. Offices and cars are obvious, but there are other, more subtle indications which can be just as damaging, and perhaps more so. These are differences in expectations and standards. What is expected of a person in a corporation usually varies a great deal according to whether that person is a worker or a manager. If, for example, a worker makes a report to the chief executive officer of the company, the CEO will almost never hold him or her to the same standard concerning presentations as he would someone from the management ranks. Perhaps unconsciously, the employee will pick up on this and understand it means he or she is a second-class citizen—with predictable results. Why should this person feel his or her interests correlate in any way with those of the company? No wonder he does not feel motivated to help the company succeed. Chances are, all he or she will do is the minimum necessary to keep a paycheck coming.

Now sit back and imagine a different world completely. Imagine how much better the business would run—how waste would be eliminated and things would hum along— if everyone in a business felt important and that their contribution mattered. Imagine if they each felt a sense of ownership and responsibility. Imagine if only one level of performance was expected from everyone—the highest possible. Imagine if all men and women inside the walls of a company were considered to be of equal value, all integral members of the same team, and all in a position to make a vital contribution. Sure, someone has to play first base, and others the outfield. Someone must take on the grueling job of catcher, and whoever has the best arm needs to pitch. But each team member's goal is to be the very best at the job he or she has, every one of which is essential in its own way. And imagine that each person knows and realizes that only if they all pull together, each performing at the peak of his or her game, will they have a chance at winning the pennant.

And what happens if they slack off and shirk their responsibilities? They get sent back to the minors. What else would make sense? As we shall see, to arrive at the high level of performance just described requires both a carrot and a stick.

**Unequal sense of ownership =
Unequal sense of commitment)**

Got Fiefdoms?

It's human nature for most people to want their own personal forty acres and a mule. And once they've got them, they'll want to add another 40 down by the river as soon as they can. Now, having latched onto 80 acres, they will likely be looking for ways to build on that, until eventually the ambitious among us will have amassed quite a fiefdom.

Because this is the way the human psyche works, and since companies are comprised of humans, most organizations tend to arrange themselves into separate internal fiefdoms, each of which is comprised of fiercely guarded turf. As a result, cooperative, integrated decision making is often absent.

I know this is true from personal experience. For many years I was a partner in a fairly large advertising agency. You cannot imagine how jealously guarded the fiefdoms were. There was the media planning department, the media buying department, account service, and marketing services and production, all of which had jobs to do and cursed be he who overstepped another department's boundaries. But the most jealously guarded fiefdom in one particular agency was the creative department. Made up of admittedly-talented art directors and copy writers with highly-elevated self esteem, the very idea someone other than a "creative" person might even occasionally have a good idea was consistently and methodically put down. So tall were the walls of the creative department fiefdom, and so fiercely were they guarded, an entire department called "traffic," with a complicated and bureaucratic system for moving the work along, insulating the "creatives" from everyone else. Looking back I realize this was its sole purpose. These "creatives" were regarded as golden-egg-laying geese to be protected from pressures or influences that otherwise might arise from clients or account [customer] service people whose job it was to see that the work got done on time, on budget, and on target. What a bottleneck this created. It took months, often with a great deal of rework, to accomplish what otherwise might have been done in a few days or even hours in a healthy, open environment.

Of course, not all companies are divided into rigorously guarded fiefdoms. But those that are usually have leaders who assume total responsibility for everything they can get their hands on. They have a "fix-it" mentality and tend to be reactive, stressed out, isolated, and tightly focused on controlling everything. Those not in management—manufacturing businesses call them "direct labor"—are the robot followers with one-skill expertise whose work is watched by a separate inspection organization. These workers are not personally involved in the company and are not concerned about output. They are not particularly concerned about quality, either, because someone else—the quality inspector—is responsible. In such a set up, supervisors tend to be dictatorial and highly reactive because they don't have time to be proactive. They spend their effort making sure every single thing is going right, as well they should. If they don't, it won't. It's actually quite strange, if you think about it. They must make sure people do what they have been hired to do.

In such an organization, the engineering department is usually very process-design oriented. Engineering does all capacity analyses, writes all standard operating procedures, and has total approval control. They certainly don't take valuable time to go to line operators, material handlers, or anyone else to consult on what might be the best way to accomplish a particular task. They just keep on churning out technical procedures and change processes without interfacing with anyone.

In such an outfit, the materials department expedites,

runs around, and tries to make sure that the product gets out. They do all the scheduling, but it is short-term scheduling because they, too, spend so much time simply reacting, and have little time for planning ahead. They are supposed to focus on production, but the truth is their knowledge of the production process often is quite limited. Maximum effort is directed toward controlling their inventory.

The same conditions can often be found in service businesses. And though differences exist from one to the next, the outcome is the same.

Focus on turf protection and individual territory creates an environment with little or no integration or communication, no shared knowledge, and little or no flexibility. This is certainly true in many of the advertising agencies I've come in contact with, worked for, and even run. Heaven forbid someone in client service should stick his nose into what the creative department considers its domain. Worst of all, even though all these people are supposed to be working toward one aim and supporting each other and the output of the firm, they often end up with entirely different objectives and goals. For creative personnel it's to win that next big award. Or, you might hear them say, "Don't let the client change that ad, I want it for my book." You see, their "book"—or portfolio—is what they use to get the next big job and more pay. If the client makes his logo bigger, this will, in the creative person's opinion, destroy the symmetry of the ad. For account service people, the driving motivation is to keep the client happy at all costs or the client will have their heads. Instead of harmony, they're fighting against each other and the overall objective of the company, which should be to make a profit by helping clients sell more goods. They are all much too concerned with their own little fiefdoms and personal objectives to worry about that.

But it doesn't have to be this way, as we shall see.

Recap

- Many companies, both in manufacturing and in service businesses, are divided into two camps: managers and workers. The "us versus them" atmosphere this creates greatly inhibits productivity.
- Companies organized in the traditional hierarchy pyramid tend to become divided into internal fiefdoms that often work at cross purposes, pursuing contradictory goals. As a result, much counterproductive time and energy is spent that could be used to advance a company's overall objectives and mission.

Chapter Two: How Things Can Be

People who don't know about the lean movement and what it entails often assume it simply means doing more with less. They think this is accomplished by having everyone work harder. They are wrong, although a 2005 survey indicates most American workers could fit in a lot more work each day. Conducted by America Online and Salary.com, it says the average worker wastes 2.09 hours each day surfing the Internet, chatting with co-workers, running errands, or making personal phone calls. That lost time costs employers about $759 billion a year in unproductive salaries.

People not only waste time on personal, non-work-related activities, some of what they do in their jobs is likely to be unproductive and unnecessary. It's not surprising, then, that the goal of going lean is to eliminate this waste. The core idea is to purge any activity or expense that does not add value to a product or service in the minds of customers, or directly generate sales at an acceptable ROI (Return on Investment). Personal activities fall into this category, of course. But there are usually plenty of things workers routinely do, which their companies even sanction or require, that could be eliminated. For example, moving parts received from suppliers in and out of storage takes time and effort—and time and effort costs money. But does it add value to the end product? Of course not. So arrangements are made with suppliers to deliver parts as they are needed, or "Just in Time" (JIT), so they can be used right away rather than put in storage only to be pulled out later. Barriers between departments and management layer upon management layer certainly do not add value. Neither does all the bureaucratic red tape that results.

An "us versus them" mentality between workers and management obviously is counterproductive, too, so everything possible is done to eliminate this and to build an atmosphere in which each individual is a key player on the same winning team. We will cover a number of ways.

Simply put, more is done with less by having everyone work smarter. Do they work harder, too? Maybe. But according to published data, people who work in true lean enterprises are significantly happier with their jobs on average than those who work in traditional businesses. Why? A fundamental reason is they are empowered to make decisions rather than to wait for some higher up to pronounce judgment on the course of action to be taken. So people have more control over their jobs and their destinies.

Just What Is a Lean Enterprise?

Lean enterprises are distinguished by six key attributes: The workplace is safe, brightly lit, orderly, and immaculately clean. Products are produced on a just-in-time basis, only to customer demand (not to forecast). Products are made in continuous flow production lines which are scheduled according to customer demand using pull-scheduling techniques.

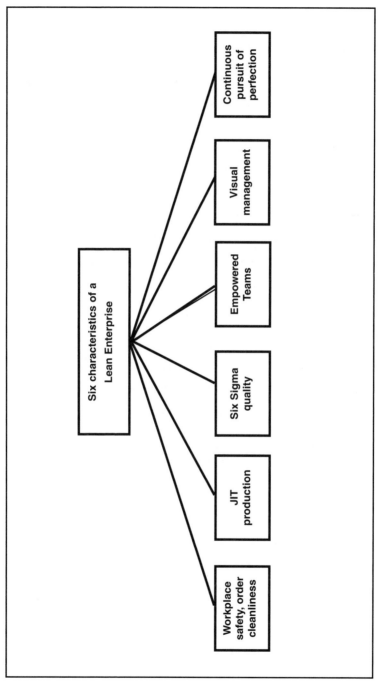

The highest quality possible (Six Sigma) is built into products and processes, not inspected in. Equipment is programmed to detect defects, and operators will shut down a production line for quality reasons. Mistake proofing is used extensively. Root cause problem solving skills are finely honed.

In traditional factories, if someone on the shop floor is asked who is responsible for quality, the answer will likely be, "our quality inspector." If the same question is asked in a lean factory, the operators will invariably say they themselves are responsible. Each person is responsible for his or her own work so it becomes each individual's responsibility to produce products without defects. The result is that the number of quality inspectors can be reduced to zero. They aren't needed because every employee is an "inspector." Everyone looks out for defects, and calls attention to them when they appear. Similarly, design engineers and process engineers will take ownership of quality. It is their job to build quality into the design and into the process.

Teams of individuals on the shop floor in the case of a manufacturing operation, or wherever value for customers is being created in a service business, are empowered to make key decisions. When a problem is spotted, the team decides how to fix it. There is no need to call in management.

In an assembly operation, for example, workers are obligated to stop the line if they see a quality defect problem. The line remains shut until the problem is fixed. This would be unthinkable in most assembly plants. Only the general manager could authorize such an action.

Command and Control Layers of a Traditional Enterprise

Operations

General Manager

Plant Manager

Production Manager

Shift Managers

Supervisors

Lead Hands

Employees

Support Services

Functional Managers

Department Managers

Supervisors

Employees

One result of operating through empowered teams is that the lean enterprise is less hierarchal than traditional businesses. No need exists for layers of supervisors, group supervisors, department heads and so forth leading up a pyramid to the person at the top. A bureaucracy would impede teams and render on-the-spot decision making impossible. Traditional hierarchies usually are not only cumbersome and slow to act, they are costly. Like any and everything that does not add value, in the lean enterprise, the goal is their elimination.

In manufacturing facilities, visual management techniques are used extensively. Management is by sight, not only by computer.

In every department and area of a lean organization from the Chairman's office to the shipping department, there is relentless pursuit of waste reduction. "Simplify, simplify, simplify!" is the battle cry.

Continuous improvement never ends in a lean enterprise. The core idea is that any and every activity or expense is to be eliminated that does not, in the view of the end user, add value. This includes all functions and processes wherever they may be, not just unnecessary or redundant work on the factory floor. Elimination of inventory, for example, is especially critical since inventory tends to hide manufacturing and distribution bottlenecks that need to be identified and opened up. Moving goods, parts and components in and out of storage is considered a waste of time and money.

Lean enterprises enjoy a number of strategic advantages over their mass manufacturing competitors. First, a lean producer is typically the low-cost producer in its industry. This allows the lean enterprise to set the market price, as lean-producer Dell Computer has done in the PC world. What makes a lean producer low cost? Lean manufacturing often requires half the space and 25 to 40 percent less direct labor than mass manufacturing. Inventory is often cut to two or three days supply, freeing up huge sums of money that would otherwise be tied up, along with enormous amounts of space previously required for storage. In the high tech arena in particular, inventory that sits in a warehouse for any length of time before it is sold may end up being a worth a lot less than it was the day it was made.

What else? Because of techniques like poke yoke [Japanese for "mistake proofing"] and worker responsibility for output quality, lean producers turn out high quality products. With defects virtually eliminated, customers are happy with what they receive. Next, back orders become a thing of the past. Using what's called "pull scheduling," lean producers make what a customer wants when he wants it, so users get what they want, and they get it fast. For example, Dell Computer uses pull scheduling, which means the company does not make a computer until an order for one is in hand. Then they make it fast, configured it just the way the customer wants, and have it delivered it to that person's door, usually within 36 hours.

This leads to what may be the biggest strategic advantage of lean—speed. Speed is the hallmark of a lean enterprise in several ways: speed of delivery of product that's configured as customers want it, speed with new product introductions, speed in management decision-making because the organization is flat and bureaucracy almost nonexistent. Speed can be a critical factor in success because a nimble organization unburdened by inventory can take full advantage of changes in the marketplace as they occur. Meanwhile, non-lean competitors will be scratching their heads, wondering what happened.

What Lean Enterprises Deliver

When all is said and done, what each of us would like when we buy a product is one that performs the tasks we want, works when it is supposed to work, costs as little as possible, and is highly reliable. We do, of course, want service if and when we need it, and we want to have our questions answered promptly and correctly. But most people don't care about guarantees or warranties, per se. What they want are no problems. Having to return something to be fixed, even at no charge, is a problem. We'd much prefer zero defects at the outset. Lean enterprises answer all those needs.

Pricing in the Global Economy

As a result of the proliferation of product choices today and of a global economy that makes competition fierce, it has become very difficult for companies to raise prices. Back in the fifties, sixties, seventies, even into the eighties, if a manufacturer's costs went up, so did its prices. The formula for setting them was "Cost + Profit = Price." No wonder inflation raised its ugly head immediately if the economy overheated. But that's much less likely to happen today. With so much variety to choose from, with so much information on what is available and where to find it because of the Internet, with so much being produced by so many companies all over the world, if the cost of an item goes up, consumers quickly substitute another in its place. This is a major reason why it is difficult to make price increases stick. In many cases, prices actually are headed down, particularly in the computer and electronics field. But this isn't the only place. As I write these words, Ford and General Motors are offering cars to the public at employee discount rates and adding rebates to boot. Other car manufacturers are beginning to offer big discounts, too, in what may be shaping up to be a price war of huge proportions.

The new equation is "Cost = Price - Profit," meaning that the marketplace sets a price. In other words, manufacturing costs and SG&A (Sales, General and Administrative Costs) are driven by the price the market is willing to pay, minus the company's desired profit on an item. In addition, it is becoming increasingly apparent that in today's economy a company must constantly lower its costs to remain competitive. The most effective and sustainable way to do this is through lean transformation and the constant pursuit of perfection. In the future, mass manufacturing and organizing a business in a traditional hierarchy simply will not allow a company to compete.

The Need for a Championship Mentality

In Chapter One we took a look at the atmosphere that exists in many businesses that operate under the old hierarchal "us versus them" way of doing business. A lean enterprise treats everyone as equally-valuable team members.

Have you ever been a player, or even the bench warmer, on a championship sports team? Then you know that it's the team that counts, not particular individuals. Indeed, a championship team functions as a single living organism, rather than as a group of separate personalities who have been thrown together. Championship players can recite the play book in their sleep. When game day arrives, every player knows his job. When the whistle blows, each takes appropriate actions that work together like the maneuvers of a precision drill team. A team such as this might be compared to an athlete who has devoted considerable time and energy climbing the Stairmaster, pumping iron, and walking the treadmill. Each cell in his body knows its place and the job that it needs to do within the greater whole. It proudly pulls its weight. The dawdlers, fat cells for instance, have long since been expunged.

How does this relate to the lean organization? If you have ever walked into an organization of people who know all the way down who they are and what they are about, you probably experienced the same sense of confidence and esprit d'corps found in the locker room of a championship team. The feeling can be palpable.

Individuals who comprise such a group don't define themselves in terms of the role they are playing on any given day. Just as the particular position played does not adequately describe a member of a championship sports team, titles do not define the members of a lean organization. Titles can be changed or be taken away. Lean players and champions are defined from the inside out. Moreover, the boundaries between departments and functions in the lean enterprise are blurred to the point that for all practical purposes they do not exist. Nor does any tolerance for a "not my job" attitude.

A person who has fully bought into the concept of lean enterprise has bought into a mind set that compels the continuous pursuit of excellence in order to advance the mission of the organization. The lean player knows a particular job that needs to be done today or next week contributes to the bigger task of what the company is about, which is to be the best.

Lean players recognize that even mundane tasks are absolutely necessary and must be executed with care and efficiency. They must be carried out professionally because, as in the case of a masterpiece, the smallest details combine to create the whole.

One thing is certain. If a task does not, or will not add value to what the company is creating, it should be eliminated. Such a task is muda [Japanese for "waste"], and worthy only of contempt. It is unseemly and useless fat.

Even a task that adds value to the end product cannot define the lean organization team member, any more than a position can define a world class soccer player. Just as "goalie" or "wing" does not do justice in describing a World Cup champion, lean organization players cannot be adequately defined as traffic managers, marketing representatives, insertion machine operators, or sales engineers. The lean player and the champion, even though they currently may occupy positions of traffic manager and goalie, are defined by the total organization of which they are a part.

An engineer at a lean company, for example, may be employed in the activity of designing circuit boards. He may even have the title, Chief Engineer, Computer Memory Chip Division. But as a lean player, it is unlikely this would be his personal definition of himself. It is more likely he would view himself as a member of a team dedicated to "serving the community by providing products and services of superior quality at a fair price." Likewise, a Wal-Mart employee who has bought into what the company is about will not define himself or herself as a checkout clerk. This individual will find self worth in existing "to provide value to our customers," just as the Nordstrom sales representative may see his role as offering "service to the customer above all else." If the authors of the best-selling book, *Built to Last,* are correct, a Sony product manager may see herself as being engaged in a worthwhile struggle "to elevate the Japanese culture and national status," and the Walt Disney worker as being part of an effort to "bring happiness to millions."

Workers in a lean enterprise, from the top of the organization to the bottom, know what they stand for because they know what the group they belong to stands for. It is the reason they are in business. This may be the single most important factor in the success of market leaders in general, no matter in what industry they operate. According to the authors of *Built to Last*, the right culture may be more important than superb products, or good ideas, or technological innovation. They theorize that employees of companies that come to dominate their industries know what they're about is producing products and services that make useful and important contributions to the lives of customers. Indeed, great products are not what make the organization outstanding. It's the other way around. The organization is what creates great products.

How does a company become an outstanding organization? How does one acquire a winning culture? We will explore techniques for fostering a team atmosphere. But even though shared goals and employee bonding may be important, they are not all that will be required.

Some companies were founded by leaders who themselves had a winning attitude and were able to instill this in subordinates. But for every one of these, there's another that was able to acquire a championship mind set along the way. I suspect that top executives going off to mountain retreats and mulling over core ideologies the company might adopt is not the only way to achieve a championship mentality. Let's consider the Green Bay Packers. This team has an illustrious heritage and has fielded more than its fair share of championship teams. But not always. Between the time of coach Vince Lombardi and the mid 1990s, the franchise slid downhill pretty far. For example, they posted four wins and twelve losses in 1988. The team needed to pull itself out of the dumps, and they did. In 1996, they won the Superbowl. How?

Let's say the desire was there. Let's say the team possessed the raw talent and the esprit d'corps. Perhaps, one essential ingredient had been missing. How does a team, or a company, come from last place to win the league championship, or to achieve dominant market share, in a few short years?

The answer is that sports teams and businesses both need to master the basics before they can achieve greatness. They must have them down pat, and this takes discipline. Only when they are in top shape, and have the fundamentals honed, will they be able to succeed in a big way.

Recap

- The basic tenet of a lean enterprise is to eliminate any activity or expense that does not add value to what the company offers, from the customer's perspective.
- There are six pillars of a lean enterprise: (1) Safety, order, cleanliness, (2) JIT production, (3) Six sigma quality built in, (4) Empowered teams, (5) Visual management, and (6) The constant pursuit of perfection.

- Quality inspectors aren't needed in a lean enterprise because of mistake proofing, designing quality in, and because each person is responsible for his or her own work.

- Lean enterprises are organized into teams. A team member who encounters a problem is expected to put his head together with others on the team and solve it.

- Because lean enterprises operate via empowered teams, bureaucratic hierarchies are eliminated.

- Cost, quality, speed, and agility are major advantages lean enterprises have over traditionally-run competitors.

- The formula for setting a price used to be: "Cost + Profit = Price." In the new global economy it's: "Cost = Price — Profit." Nowadays, the marketplace sets the price. A business that wants to survive must meet it.

- Lean enterprises work as one team, not separate fiefdoms.

Chapter Three: Setting the Stage for Change

Traditional manufacturers operate in batch and queue mode. Work is done, perhaps the milling of a part or the creation of one. These parts pile up in batches until they are taken to the next stage of production, where they wait to be used. This method of production is viewed as wasteful since batches take up space and tie up money. On a balance sheet they are called "work-in-progress." Plus, no one can know if the parts in a particular batch will fit correctly until an operator begins trying to insert them.

To eliminate these issues, lean factories are organized into continuously flowing lines from the initial production step all the way to the shipping dock. Think of a number of individual streams, or tributaries, that flow together to form a river with no dams along the way. This method is called "continuous flow," or lean production, and it's usually the first step taken in the transformation to lean of a manufacturing business.

The same principle can be applied in a service business. The place where value is created for customers should be reworked so that a customer's experience is the best it can possibly be in terms of speed and service. There should be no wasted motion, no unnecessary steps. If something does not enhance the customer's experience, it needs to go. But simply streamlining may not always be the answer. Sometimes the best solution is an entirely new way of going about the task of creating customer value. An example can be found in the book Bruce Goldman and I co-wrote called *Lean Advertising.* Bruce and I developed a process for creating advertising using the principles Toyota employs to design new cars, which is to go about the activity in a non-linear way. Rather than turn the development of an ad campaign over to an art director and a copy writer to mull over, take coffee breaks, and push pencils around for a couple of weeks, our method is to employ a cross-functional team to generate a plethora of possible ad campaign directions—as many as can be said to be on strategy. Once half dozen people from different disciplines with different personalities and different backgrounds are together in a room, this process takes only a few hours at most. You should see the concepts pour forth once people get going and rev up. Afterward, these ideas are reviewed and some may be refined by our creative director. The really stupid ones tossed out. What's left is usually a dozen or more ideas worthy of further consideration. And instead of weeks, the entire process takes at most a couple of days. At this point, we involve the client in what becomes a combination brainstorming and narrowing process.

Our experience has been that ad campaigns not only are developed in a fraction of the time the old way required, they are much more "creative" than they used to be. Clients are happy. We are happy.

By the way, if you work in an "information" business, I highly recommend the book where we got many of our ideas. It is called *Product Development for the Lean Enterprise:*

Why Toyota's System is Four Times More Productive and How You Can Implement It by Michael N. Kennedy.

So there you are. First you work on the area of the business where customer value is created. You purge it of waste and make it the best it can be. After it is transformed, lean thinking is spread throughout the entire organization to eliminate wasted motion wherever it's found. Eventually a lean organization comes to be—at least in theory.

Experience has shown this to be more difficult than you might imagine. In fact, it isn't likely to happen without a definite plan that includes the steps to be taken to get from here to there.

Five Key Factors for Lean Enterprise Success

It's been my experience and that of others who have taken part in successful lean transformations that five factors are required for a successful, ongoing transformation:

(1) *Top management* (the *primary team* in a lean enterprise) *must have a strategic vision of what the organization is moving toward and will become.* This team must be able to see how the company will be different, and what, for example, the primary advantages over competition will be. This strategic vision must be held firmly in mind, and communicated to leaders and staff throughout the organization so that it becomes a shared vision all are working toward.

(2) *Strong line leadership people should be selected by the primary team as change agents.* They will head cross-functional teams that guide the transformation. It's essential

these individuals must be committed to change. Leaders of the transformation must be chosen carefully. They must have the imagination necessary to grasp "what can be," and share the primary team's vision of the company's future. An important aspect of the makeup of leaders selected to institute change should be that they focus on the future and the possibilities it holds, rather than on the past and its time-honored traditions.

(3) *Expert training and support likely will be needed in order to get started.* This may require bringing in a seasoned lean transformation expert to help in at least the initial, start up and training phase. After training has taken place, those left in charge should have enough knowledge to be self-correcting in the event that the transformation strays off course. It also may help to have a sounding board, some-one who has been through transformation, who can be called upon periodically for advice and counsel.

(4) *Aggressive lean enterprise performance targets and track-ing.* People need to know what is expected of them, and they need goals and objectives to shoot for. This might take the form of specific objectives to do with reductions in throughput time, inventory turns, scrap reduction, and returns due to defects. Goals in general can be important motivators and will form a major topic of discussion in this section.

(5) *Impatience by management to see the organization move ahead and deliver tangible results.* Impatience means that foot-dragging will not be tolerated. It means that what we will learn are referred to as "concrete heads" will not be given

much time to get on board. In its most productive form, impatience should translate into a fire that is lit under the organization to realize the vision.

Indeed, many have discovered what is now referred to as "The Lean Enterprise Paradox." This is that management must be simultaneously directive and empowering. It would seem that these traits do not go hand in hand. But experience has revealed that strong leadership is required; leadership that is unambiguous, leadership that is clear about the lean enterprise path. At the same time, a leader must continually empower teams along the way. Teams must be handed complete authority to carry out assigned tasks. Those who would block progress by trying to hold on to the old hierarchy—their turf—and perpetuate an "us versus them" mentality need to be converted. They deserve a chance to move through he five stages of change acceptance—denial, anger, bargaining, depression, acceptance—but they cannot be allowed to hold up progress long. There may come a point if they are stuck in stage one, two, three, or four when the only intelligent course will be to turn them out to pasture.

EXPERIENCE SHOWS that when the five lean enterprise factors are present, and obstructionists have been removed, impressive results will be achieved. But if one or more factors are missing, a company's lean transformation is likely to fail to live up to expectations.

A word of caution is appropriate. Impatience, while needed and potentially constructive, should be tempered with a healthy dose of realism. An important decision to make is how quickly to move ahead once a lean transformation has begun. In manufacturing and assembly operations, this will depend largely on the ability of the supporting infrastructure to keep up. If one or two lines are all that's involved, infrastructure may not be an issue. But the situation can be considerably different if there are 6, 10, 20, or more assembly lines in a given complex. Maintenance and material handling are likely to become stressed as the conversion of one line after another takes place.

Factor Number One: A Strategic Vision

Here is an important question for the top leader of an organization to ask and answer. Knowing what you now know about lean enterprise, what would you want your company to look like if you were starting today from scratch? If you were running a computer company, for example, would your vision be that of Dell, with its continuous flow to customer pull method of supply, manufacturing, and distribution, or would it be modeled after one of the more traditionally run computer sales and assembly businesses?

The business section of my local newspaper lies next to my computer this July 2005 morning as I key in these words. A headline says Hewlett-Packard Company has just announced it will be cutting 14,500 jobs over the next 18 months. HP CEO Mark Hurd is quoted as saying, "Our objective is to create a simpler, nimbler HP with . . . clear accountability and greater financial flexibility." Guess I'll have to send him a copy of this book, as well as one of Henderson and Larco's *Lean Transformation: How to Change Your Business into a Lean Enterprise,* which goes into some detail contrasting the business models of Dell and Hewlett-Packard.

Ask and answer this. How does the Dell model translate into your industry? How would you set it up?

This may well be your vision.

TO REALIZE this vision will require dramatic change, and change can be difficult. It can be frightening for those who find comfort in the known and the expected, even when the known and expected are not all that wonderful. Maybe this is why incumbent politicians often have a big advantage over challengers. Given this reality, how can a leader get people to accept the new vision? What will get their attention and blast them out of complacency?

One catalyst can be a real or perceived crisis. It might be your company no longer is able to compete effectively. Let's look directly into the eyes of reality. Over time, organizations can become over staffed. Positions that once served a useful purpose may become outmoded by changes in technology or the marketplace. Yet the people who fill them remain on the payroll. Unless you happen to be starting an organization from scratch, it is very likely your organization has too much fat, too much waste, too many workers, too much duplication and too much equipment devoted to activities that do not create value. This is doubly true if a competitor happens to adopt a course of lean transformation. If a company has not yet reached a state of crisis, its leaders would be wise to consider trumping one up. If they wait, they will likely face a real crisis later that will be nearly impossible to overcome. Not long ago as of this writing, for example, General Motors announced a major reorganization entailing the elimination of thousands of jobs. If it were not for the magnitude of this overhaul, it's doubtful the story would have created headlines at all, at least not in newspapers beyond the company's headquarters city, Detroit. In this new age of global competition, only those companies offering the highest quality at the lowest prices will survive.

If your company happens to be in what appears to be a do-or-die position, you may actually be fortunate and not yet realize it. An opportunity has presented itself. A catalyst for change is at your fingertips, one that will light a fire under every manager and worker who wants to remain gainfully employed. Lean enterprise is a survival strategy they should thankfully embrace, a potential lifesaver they cannot afford to reject. Once they see it this way, most will pull together to do what's necessary to make the transformation, and the odds are excellent the company will emerge stronger and more competitive.

What if your business doesn't face an immediate crisis? What if the transformation is primarily a defensive measure to remain competitive, or an offensive measure to strengthen the company's position? Opposition will be strong, not from workers, but from middle management.

Those who have been through a transformation will tell

you the attitudes of workers will likely change from somber or glum to enthusiastic and upbeat in a matter of days or weeks. Post transformation surveys indicate they often believe that they aren't working as hard afterward as they did before. Employee job satisfaction usually soars. Workers feel empowered because they are.

Factor Number Two: Strong Line Leadership

Strong line leadership—those chosen as team leader change agents—is absolutely critical to a successful lean enterprise program. Without their full commitment, failure is almost certain. As has been discussed, becoming a lean enterprise involves major cultural change, and this requires perseverance. And cultural and technical roadblocks are not all that must be cleared away. Floor layouts, people, multiple levels of bureaucracy, systems such as accounting and MRP, all will have to be changed. The truth is, lean enterprise "goes against the grain" of just about everything companies have held dear since the days of Henry Ford's first assembly lines.

This is one of the most critical lessons learned: The inertia factor of a traditional manufacturer cannot be underestimated. For those who do not want to change, it will be a classic case of, "You can lead a horse to water, but you can't make him drink." The truth is, more than inertia is at work. The traditional organization will fight back.

Let's say a successful kaizen* event is held with huge

---

* In a Kaizen event, workers are brought together to brainstorm and implement ways to eliminate waste and improve productivity.

improvements in performance. Enthusiasm will be high among the participants. They will be charged up and ready to find more ways to improve. This is probably the moment a backlash from the traditional organization will occur.

Why? Turf has been threatened. Consider, for example, the copy writers and art directors at an ad agency that's gone lean. Do you think they will like the idea of a brainstorming session made up of a cross-functional team doing in a couple of hours the job it used to take them two or three weeks to do? Of course not.

In a factory that's gone lean, it's the old supervisors who are likely to rebel. You can expect them to complain that, to the great detriment of the company, control and discipline have been lost. A "tug of war" between early adapters and what many have called "concrete heads" will ensue. About 80% of the organization will be caught smack in the middle. The outcome will either be success or failure, and this will depend on the actions taken by team-leader change agents.

This leads to what was referred to a short time ago as the "Lean Enterprise Paradox." Line management style must be directive *and* empowering.

The words "directive" and "empowering" do not sound as if they ought to go together. In this case they do. Strong leadership is required, leadership that is crystal clear about the lean enterprise path and on board with it. At the same time, the top leaders in the organization must continually empower the teams along the way. The best advice is not to waste time with people who will not change. Moreover, be aware that you have a big problem on your hands if many of your plant managers falls into this category, and and even bigger one if you have a concrete head in a general manager position. All probably will have to be replaced, or transformation at the plant level will be stifled. Even if everyone else other than these leaders wants to change, the effort will fail.

Factor Number Three: Expert Training and Support

Expert training and support will likely be required in order for you to get going, especially if little lean enterprise experience exists in your company. You may have to bring in someone from the outside to help with this.

But don't go overboard. You will need enough to get started, and enough knowledge on site on an ongoing basis to be self-correcting when a false step or a mistake is made.

Where does the required lean expertise come from? Typically, it comes from people already on staff, as well as new hires who have prior experience with lean. It can also come from an outside consultant.

It makes sense to begin the transformation in the area closest to the customer. In manufacturing, this is final assembly. Begin the training program with the personnel who work in this area. A major goal is to develop a "picture" of a lean producer in their minds.

Factor Number Four: Aggressive Performance Targets

Measurements are important in tracking lean enterprise implementation. They can be designed to take advantage of existing plant-level data and to minimize the amount of additional information to be collected and might include inventory turns, the number of defects per thousand (customer PPM), on-time-delivery (OTD) to customer want dates, and financial performance measures such as SG&A (Sales, General & Administrative overhead). The book by Jorge Larco and Bruce Henderson which I edited called *Lean Transformation* goes into detail on the various types of metrics that might be tracked.

Factor Number Five: Impatience

Impatience should lead the lean enterprise leader to take action when he or she begins hearing, "You don't understand. We are different." Or, "If we do that, it will disrupt the organization." Impatience means that concrete heads will not be given much time to get on board.

Top leaders need to take at least a daily walk through the organization. They need to hand out positive strokes where progress is apparent, and express displeasure with a lack of results.

The primary (top) team in an organization should demonstrate impatience by regularly reviewing progress and action reports (which will be discussed later), and make it known they know exactly where things stand. A positive trend, or the lack of one, should be noted. If you move too slowly in transforming to lean, valuable momentum and enthusiasm can be lost. If you move too quickly, inevitable glitches, and in manufacturing businesses the inability of materials supply and maintenance to keep up, can give naysayers gasoline to pour on the fire of discontent. Count on it. There will be naysayers.

Communications

Communications can play an important role in helping the organization jell and rally to accomplish the lean transformation. So leaders should use every tool they can, from newsletters, to strategy documents, to brochures, videos and advertising, in order to spread the word and turn up the heat. Nothing makes something so real as putting it in writing. An ad or story in your industry's trade journal that talks about your going lean signals that you're deadly serious, not only to customers, but to employees. So what if your competitors find out what you're up to—in the spirit of Toyota, why worry? By the time they're able to copy you, if they even try, you'll be light years ahead of them.

Recap

Five factors are required to insure a successful lean transformation:
- The primary team (top management) must have a

clear vision of how the organization will look when the transformation is complete.

- Strong and committed team leaders down the line must be selected by the primary team and empowered as change agents.
- Outside training and support will likely be needed.
- Aggressive performance targets should be set and tracked.
- Impatience should be displayed when necessary by the top leader in the business.

Chapter Four: Getting Started

The management of some companies decide to allow natural attrition take care of the reduction in staff that will be required to run the business once it is lean. Others do not have this luxury or don't wish to wait. If your transformation is conducted simultaneously with a downsizing of the organization, the best way to begin is to have a hard look at the role each position plays in the company to determine its purpose and effectiveness. The goal is to evaluate every box on the organization chart in terms of activities connected with it that add value for customers, or deliver sales. Any activities that do not should be scratched. Some positions are likely to be eliminated entirely and activities from many folded into others.

Often organizations have large corporate support staffs. Many of these positions can be eliminated or assigned to the appropriate business unit.

If an activity doesn't logically fit into a unit, it should be eliminated as a redundant service. One company I worked with had a corporate engineering staff that did work for a number of business units. This was eliminated and a policy instituted that whatever engineering a unit needed had to be done by that unit, and the unit had to pay for it. Another had corporate ad managers who worked with divisions. What was the point? The divisions were perfectly capable of getting their own advertising done.

In some cases it may be possible to eliminate redundancy by having business units work more closely together. Take engineering at General Motors, for example, where walls and fiefdoms apparently were rampant until recently. Each business in each part of the world developed its cars independently, creating a huge amount of redundant work in design engineering. According to published reports, a change is underway that is resulting in each region taking the lead in developing platforms and parts for specific vehicle types. North America will engineer luxury cars and most trucks and SUVs. Europe will take the lead on compact and midsize cars. Australia will develop the underpinnings of some rear-drive cars, and GM's Korean Daewoo operations will work on subcompact cars and small SUVs. James E. Queen, vice-president for global engineering was quoted as saying, "The big change is that these engineers are working on behalf of GM, not their specific region." Engineers at GM Daewoo Auto & Technology Company in Korea are already working on the next Saturn Vue small SUV for the U.S. market. New virtual-engineering tools let American designers see a life-size 3D image of the Vue on a wall-size screen in GM's design studio in Detroit. Design changes can be discussed via speakerphone between executives in Detroit and Korean engineers who are looking at the same image. By better meshing its global operations, GM hopes to wring out costs and then pump the savings into better models.

Corporate marketing is another area where big savings can often be realized without sacrificing quality or effectiveness. It's not unusual for a large company to have a dozen different ad agencies working on different projects and brands. Why not have each agency submit an RFQ (Request for Quote) to do all the work, or at least a large portion of it. Consolidating with one agency, or even just a few, may eliminate a lot of duplication of effort and save a big wad of money. The same situation may exist with other multiple suppliers. If you are looking to save the company money every place you can, the supply chain being one of them, let me recommend a great book by Patricia E. Moody called, *The Big Squeeze: Ten Ways to Cut Your Spend 10% Right Now.*

Look Inside Each Business Unit

Identifying redundancies between corporate staff and business unit staff isn't difficult, but identifying redundancies within business units can be. Some management consultants offer computer programs that allow every job in the company to be outlined, including where the job is located and the responsibilities assigned to it. Individuals are not identified, nor should they be, only the positions they fill. This allows a leader to see where activities might exist in more than one place at the same time. The heads of each business unit can then be questioned about each position and why it is necessary. They are asked if overlapping responsibilities can be reassigned, and if not, why not. In this way positions can be realigned and many eliminated. Then individuals can be reassigned. Usually, the head count can be reduced dramatically as a result.

As mentioned, the best strategy is one that requires every job in the company to have a tie or a connection to customers. Either it adds value, or it creates sales. The question must then be asked and answered, what return is generated by this activity? If the return isn't there, it should be eliminated.

How the New Organization Will Look

Let's say you've got the five factors in place and you've identified positions to be eliminated. How should the new organization look? How are you going to get things done without the old hierarchy of supervisors and reports? The answer is interlocking teams.

Every person in the business should be on a home team whether they are the CEO or a worker on the loading dock. Membership is not optional. Many will be on a home team they lead, and on another team as a member. For example, the head of manufacturing at an industrial plant will be the leader of a team made up of the leaders of each production line team, and he will have membership status on the primary team headed by the plant manager—along with team leaders from engineering, marketing, material supply, and other disciplines that operate from the plant. While some teams such as this cross-functional home team are permanent, other cross-functional teams made up of representatives of different disciplines may be formed to address specific tasks or to take on a particular project. Once the project is completed, the team will disband.

**Rather than the traditional corporate pyramid,
the lean enterprise is organized of
interlocking teams,
reducing the number of layers from as many as
five or six to as little as two**

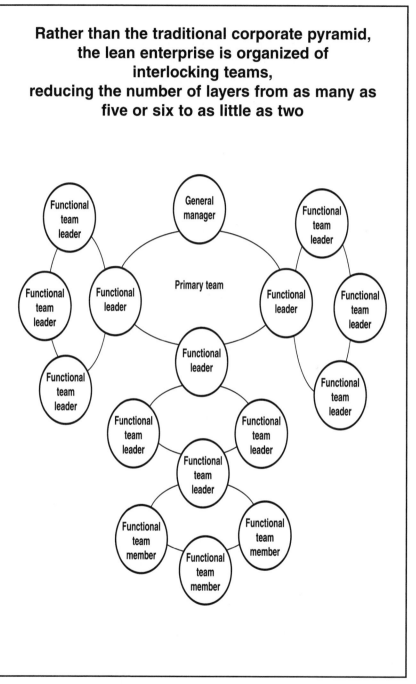

Home Teams

A home team is defined as the natural work group. This would be the boss and his or her direct reports in a traditionally structured organization. A home team may be called a unit, a cell or a department. Natural work groups function well as home teams because they are structured to focus on what they contribute to the business.

Teams facilitate communication within an organization because all teams interlock. Something decided in a primary team meeting will be taken by each member to the home team he leads, whose members will take it to the teams they lead, and so on throughout the organization.

One result of operating through empowered teams is that no need exists for layers of supervisors, group supervisors, department heads and so forth leading up a pyramid to the person at the top. A bureaucracy would impede teams and render on-the-spot decision making impossible.

Traditional hierarchies usually are not only cumbersome and slow to act, they are costly. Like any and everything that does not add value, in the lean enterprise, the goal is their elimination.

In one plant that was transformed to lean, five layers of management were between general manager and shop floor worker when the change began. The plant employed about four hundred workers, not a particularly large number, yet reporting to the general manager on the manufacturing side was a head of operations, followed by the head

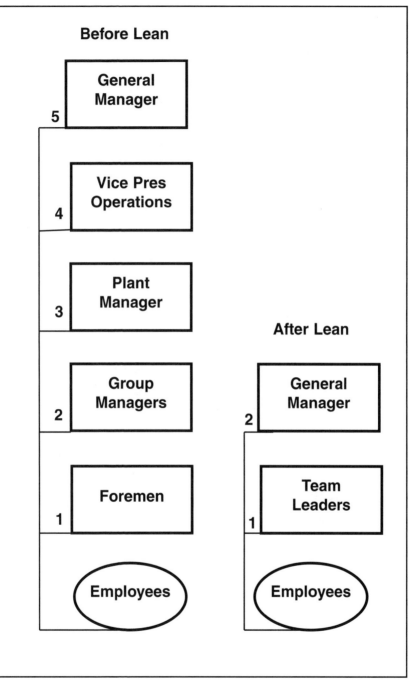

Before Lean

5 | General Manager

4 | Vice Pres Operations

3 | Plant Manager

2 | Group Managers

1 | Foremen

Employees

After Lean

2 | General Manager

1 | Team Leaders

Employees

of production, the head of the shop, a layer of supervisors, and a cadre of group leaders, with each group leader responsible for a cell of shop floor workers. This was in contrast to one of the most efficient and productive plants I've heard about which employed more than a thousand workers and had only two management levels. The first plant was changed to look like the second.

Moving from Hierarchy to Flat

Let's say you decide to move to interlocking teams and deep six the hierarchy. How do all the details of work flow and procedures get put in place? The primary team needs to appoint a cross-functional team made up of leaders from each discipline to work them out. Each appointee will in turn choose a team of individuals from his or her respective area to provide input. Input teams will meet and work out ways the new system might work. The leaders will bring these recommendations to the cross-functional team meeting, which will in turn develop a list of options to be considered in milestone meetings of the full organization. This process will be discussed at greater length in the chapter headed "Making Change Happen."

The appointed leaders who form this cross-functional team must be strong and passionately share the top leader's vision of what the new organization will look like. Individually, they should be respected throughout the business for the skill and talent they bring to their own respective functions.

Choosing Change Agents

Care needs to be taken by the primary team in choosing the leaders of this cross-functional team. Some managers have a tendency to become effective change agents and others don't. It has nothing to do with education, experience or age. Potential change agents will tend to describe themselves as "innovative," while potential concrete heads see themselves as "practical."

Potential change agents are likely to focus on the future and the possibilities it holds. The possible is always out front, pulling on their imaginations the way a magnet pulls on iron filings. The future holds more attraction for them than the past and present.

Potential concrete heads will describe themselves as being firmly grounded in reality. Like Detective Sergeant Joe Friday, they'll say they want facts. They remember facts. They also believe in experience, and sincerely think they know from experience everything that works and everything that doesn't. Potential foot draggers can never have enough facts. Once they've collected a pile, they'll want still more. Like Civil War General McClellan with troops, horses and munitions, it may seem that they can never have enough facts to go into action.

Potential change agents, on the other hand, don't make information gathering the end-all. They want and value data, but only enough of it to see a pattern, to support a hunch or theory, to justify making de Bono's intuitive leap to action

Word and Idea Preferences

Concrete heads:

- Past
- Experience
- Time-tested
- Traditional
- Facts
- Sensible
- No nonsense
- Perspiration
- Actual
- Down-to-earth

Lean change agents:

- Future
- Innovative
- Speculative
- Imaginative
- Hunches
- Possibilities
- Ingenuity
- Inspiration
- Intuition
- Theoretical

based on the pattern or coherence they see. For them, information simply "hangs together" to support a course of action. They may continue gathering data after they themselves are convinced, but only to win over potential naysayers.

Change agents tolerate established procedures but willingly abandon any that can be shown to be counterproductive or irrelevant to the goals they seemingly serve. Concrete heads, in contrast, are so in tune with established, time-honored institutions and procedures that they simply cannot understand anyone wanting to abandon or change them.

Though visionary leadership isn't part of a concrete head's makeup, they can, under normal circumstances, be effective administrators. In positions where the objective is to maintain status quo, they can even be valuable to an organization. But since lean transformation is neither normal circumstances nor devoted to maintaining the status quo, a different kind of leader is called for—one who likes looking for a better way.

This kind of change agent must be willing to step out front and take risks. He or she must be constantly on the lookout for new and better ways of doing things, stimulated by possibilities and constantly motivated by a restless feeling that there are better and more efficient ways.

Once the change agents have been selected, there must be a drop-dead, set-in-stone timetable specifying what has to happen and when the key steps towards change will take place.

How to Make Sure It Works

It makes sense to make the people who will have to live with the new vision day-to-day responsible for setting down the rules and making them work. What better incentive is there for getting things right? It will be impossible for them to point the finger at someone else if something should go awry, and if something does, they can fix what doesn't work.

After the obvious first steps of identifying and rooting out non value-added steps, the team of change agent leaders will give the rest of the organization a more concrete version of the vision and a shove in the right direction to carry it out—putting the responsibility on them to create a new system their own way. This will be done in large group sessions described in the "Mechanics of Change" chapter beginning on page 95.

The top leader has to be patient and persistent while this changeover is going on. But he or she must simultaneously be impatient. Impatient with resistance, impatient with foot-dragging, impatient with going through the motions, impatient enough to light a fire under the whole organization until it delivers tangible results.

Get Ready for Concrete Heads

A small percentage of workers—and a larger proportion of managers—will be unable or unwilling to change work habits that have become as much a part of them as their hairstyle or the clothes they wear. Later we're going to cover ways that will work to get many of them on board, but even these techniques will not on work on everyone. The extreme discomfort some will feel with the new way of working will make them do things from talking the talk but not walking the walk to willfully undermining the transformation.

This is because going from traditional to lean turns everything upside down. Instead of top-down decision-making, there's teamwork and decision-making down the line. Instead of thinking of steps and procedures first, it's customer pull that comes first. That's what makes Toyota the envy of automakers on every continent, but it's also what gives many managers nightmares. So they, more than anyone else, may need a thorough reorientation. Managers will need to know that they must let go. That they simply will no longer be in a position to give orders. That they'll have to become coaches who let workers take responsibility—even if that means shutting everything down if quality's at risk. It means everyone must work together. That the workplace must become participative instead of authoritarian, and that what's good for the business as a whole must come before what 's good for any individual.

This goes against most managers' training and experience, to say nothing of the basic human territorial instinct. When empowered teams composed of people who used to work for them take over and start hitting triples and home runs, some are going to feel, at the very least, anxious about the change and concerned that their power has been usurped. So this group is likely to start waging guerrilla warfare.

Watch Out for Unconscious Undermining

Here's one example. After weeks of planning and conversations with individuals throughout his organization about the coming transformation, the day came for a CEO to brief his entire management team on the details. Marketing, research and development, purchasing, engineering, sales and operations managers from throughout the company were gathered in a hotel ballroom. The CEO stepped forward to speak. His VP of manufacturing and other top executives flanked him on the dais. The intended message of their presence was that everyone in senior management stood behind the move. But it soon became apparent that they didn't. The VP of manufacturing had never argued about going lean, nor had he voiced any concerns. But he let the entire room know he opposed the plan by rolling his eyes and shaking his head as the CEO outlined certain actions. His body language may have been unconscious, but he clearly let everyone know where he stood. As a result, he severely undermined confidence.

In another company, an operations manager was brought into a catastrophic situation. Productivity was in the basement, expenses were through the roof, production was so backed up that customers were restive. The assembly operation, which normally ran two ten-hour shifts four days a week, was now running around the clock for five, six, sometimes seven days straight. There was so much overtime and time-and-a-half that most workers were too tired out to be interested in making more. Needless to say, the unit was in the red.

The new manager saw immediately that the organization lacked discipline, so he moved quickly to establish authority. He issued a directive that not one decision was to be made, no overtime was to be authorized, and not a purchase order was to be written without his personal approval. Noting that the assembly operation was in disarray, he hired a cadre of supervisors whose job it was to clamp down and keep a tight rein. He met with them daily and issued strict orders. He got tough, fired troublemakers and refused to put up with foolishness. He wore a scowl. Fear spread, and with it came order.

Soon, the situation was no longer out of control. Within three or four months it had stabilized. The backlog was down to a manageable level. The work week was down to four days, where it belonged. The bottom line was now slightly into the black.

This manager deserved a pat on the back, correct? Yes, and he got it. Given the state of affairs when he'd arrived, his actions may have been necessary. His techniques were old school, to say the very least, but he was able to achieve a respectable degree of success.

Then the company leadership decided that, having stabilized the organization and established discipline, the time had come to begin the transformation to lean. To reduce layers of management. To push decision-making down to line managers and assembly teams. To replace the authoritarian approach—which had served its purpose if it ever really had been necessary—with teamwork and esprit de corps and let them work.

How do you suppose the manager felt about this? As you might expect, his expression didn't resemble one of those smile emotions :-) . But he said he'd do his best. He allowed a lean enterprise consultant into the plant, and this consultant began working with one of the production-line cells. Within a couple of weeks this line had made enormous productivity gains.

Soon the operations manager was telling his subordinates to "play along" with the transformation. They were to pretend to be working toward the lean transformation—but only while top managers or the consultant were present. Then it would be back to business as usual.

Needless to say, top management was not pleased. But we can understand why he felt as he did. He'd turned around a bad situation in a short time. Even so, the line that had been transformed to continuous flow was producing at a remarkable level. Couldn't he see this?

His CEO went over the figures with him. He grudgingly acknowledged the gain. Top management decided to give him the benefit of the doubt and, with it, another chance. They applauded him for the turnaround and for doing what he felt he must to make it happen. They told him they were convinced that his plant was in position to become a showcase, but only he could make it happen. He now had a model to follow, the line that already had been converted. What was required would be to expand the transformation to the other assembly lines, and eventually throughout every area and department in his plant.

But rumors persisted that he was still sandbagging. He was told that the decision to go lean had been made at the highest level. It was going to happen; no exceptions would be allowed. His plant would have to be brought into the fold. If specified progress was not made toward the metrics which had been established as goals within six months, the company would be forced to find someone else to make it happen.

He agreed to accept the challenge, but what took place was a thorough disappointment. When the lean consultant went on to his next assignment, the operations manager dismantled all the steps toward lean production. The lean production line was returned to its traditional way of working and to its old level of productivity. Shop floor workers became disheartened and cynical. Six months after the ultimatum, the plant was still only marginally profitable. The manager was given his walking papers, and a new manager was brought in.

A Concrete Head Sees the Light

Fortunately, many managers who start out strongly opposed to change end up as strong change agents themselves. When the general manager of a fairly efficient operation that had recently been acquired in a merger first saw his new management's presentation on lean production, his body language made it obvious he wasn't a happy camper. He sat in classic defensive posture—arms folded across his chest, a frown on his face. Now and then his eyes appeared to roll back.

This man saw the same presentation a second time when it was given to his new boss and the boss's immediate subordinates. The boss was unabashedly enthusiastic, and apparently his enthusiasm did not go unnoticed.

The general manager saw the presentation a third time when it was shown to key managers at his plant. By then, his demeanor had changed. The consultant received a warm welcome. Machines were moved and several batch processes eliminated. In no time, throughput picked up.

Workers received more authority. Teams brain stormed ways to do things better. New procedures supplanted old ones.

Soon the plant's productivity, including both direct and indirect labor, had improved by 40 percent. Output was way up with the same number of workers. Payroll was down significantly because outside, part-time help was no longer needed.

Then the inevitable backlash occurred. Middle managers who felt stripped of their authority clamored to have things returned to the old way. The general manager called his staff together. He explained that the organization was not turning back. That he was committed to lean transformation. That nothing would or could stop progress.

Difficulties surely would arise in the future, he added. They, too, would be met and overcome. Anyone holding out hope that the business would revert to the old way of working would be better off to let go of that illusion and get with the program. If they didn't like the new way, and weren't willing to help make it take hold, they should start looking for another job right now.

The crisis passed. The transformation continued. Today, that shop is a model lean enterprise.

Now, both of these managers were intelligent and had been successful in their careers. Both appeared to have had good reasons to want to make lean production work. Why did one refuse to accept the concept, while the other eventually embraced it as his own? Could the general manager have been more highly motivated than the operations manager? His plant had recently changed ownership as the result of a merger. He had new owners and new bosses who obviously were enthusiastic believers in lean production. The manager was in his fifties. Finding a new job at his age might not have been easy. Yet an ultimatum was neither issued nor ever needed.

The operations manager also was in his fifties. It was obvious that his superiors, too, believed enthusiastically in lean enterprise. He was actually told he would have to find a new job if he didn't make the transition happen. Yet it appears he didn't even try.

Why?

Might he have felt more secure because of his recent successes? He had indeed turned around a bad situation. He may have believed that the goals placed before him could be met using the old, traditional way of working. I'm guessing this was the case and that he simply didn't possess the qualities of a change agent discussed earlier.

Sometimes Repetition Does the Trick

Remember the general manager who at first seemed skeptical and later embraced lean concepts? Only after seeing the same presentation on lean enterprise three times did he become a believer. That, plus his superiors' very obvious enthusiasm, was enough to open his mind. He took the ball and ran with it.

As an old advertising guy, I'm not surprised. As hundreds of thousands of dollars' worth of research has shown, repetition is often needed to get the message across. The first time someone sees something new, whether it's an ad or anything else, the usual reaction is to categorize it in terms of old knowledge. Suppose, for example, someone sees a purple cow. The reaction might be, "What's that? Oh, it's a cow, except it's purple." Once they've got this in a pigeon hole, they feel free to move on.

The second time they see the cow, their reaction is likely to be more personally evaluative. "Aha, there's that purple cow again. Odd. But what does it mean to me?"

If they decide that the purple cow has relevance for them, the third and subsequent exposures will reinforce this. They may take action after the second exposure, or many more may be required push them over the line. Our general manager, for example, got the point after the third exposure.

If, like the concrete head, someone decides that the purple cow has no relevance to them, no amount of repetition will change that person's mind. It's made up, so subsequent exposures are ignored and accomplish nothing. The lesson is repetition can be important and helpful in making converts, but only if those potential converts are predisposed to innovation, only if they have a built-in uneasiness about the status quo, and only if they're future- and possibility-oriented.

Recap

- The new organization will be built of interlocking home teams empowered to make and carry out decisions in the part of the business they represent.
- This facilitates communications and eliminates the need for a layered hierarchy.
- Fewer people will be needed. Some companies reduce to a smaller number through attrition, others through downsizing.
- The best way to downsize is to evaluate each position in terms of how or if it adds value for customers or delivers sales, scratch those that don't, and combine redundancies to eliminate positions.
- Corporate support staff should be eliminated or relocated in specific business units.
- Redundancy may be eliminated by having units work more closely together and share personnel and resources.
- Often several outside suppliers such as multiple advertising agencies can be combined to

increase buying power and reduce costs.

- Carefully selected change agents making up a cross-functional team, each headed a team he or she selects from his or her area, should lead and implement the change.
- People who will have to live with procedures day to day should decide the details of these procedures so they will embrace and own them.
- Be prepared to deal with people who refuse to shift their thinking and behavior to the new way.

Chapter Five: Preparing for Change

The basic idea of what constitutes good leadership undergoes a profound transformation when a company goes lean. In many ways, what happens resembles the theory of evolution. For example, you might say there are four distinct stages beginning with the "Neanderthal Despot," a prehistoric life form still common in corporate America, and ending with the "Championship Team Coach," the advanced leadership species of tomorrow. As individuals reach each more advanced level of evolutionary development, they become better and better leaders because they are sharing more and more responsibility with employees. Neanderthals, for example, share none, whereas Championship Team Coaches encourage widespread employee involvement in running the business. In addition, at each level managers possess different characteristics and even talk to employees differently.

The leadership transformation is also like evolution for another reason—neither one is an overnight phenomenon. It's never easy to break old habits, so everyone needs to accept that changing leadership techniques will take time and practice. Here are some qualities of effective leadership that you can start on right away.

The manager who wants to become a lean leader should begin by looking at the exhibit on page 75 and determining where he or she stands on it and start taking the corrective action needed. He or she should think back to the last few times he came face-to-face with an employee and how he handled the situation.

But let's face it, most of us don't have the gift of being able to see ourselves as others see us. A way around this is to gather together other would-be leaders who know each other well and may be in the same boat. They, too, should be familiar the chart.

The purpose of this session will be for each leader to face reality about themselves with a little help from their peers. One leader might start out by listing out loud what he thinks is his management style. He should mention as many positive and negative adjectives as possible such as responsible, consistent, thorough, domineering and short-tempered. These might be written on a marker board. His peers can then agree or disagree and add to or subtract from the list. Everyone needs to be honest with one another and tactfully tell it like it is. Would-be leaders will come out of this session with a pretty good idea of where they are and how far they have to go.

Balanced Leadership

The next step is to learn "balanced leadership." As a lean leader, a person needs to learn how to balance giving up control with taking charge. Most who have spent a career dictating orders to employees, often have some difficulty stepping back and cheering them on.

But balanced leadership doesn't mean becoming a virtual cheerleader who spends the entire game on the side-

Stages of Leadership Evolution

Championship team coach

- Monitor
- Trainer
- People driven
- Seeks consensus

Homo sapien

- Delegator
- Group coach
- Change agent

Cro-magnon

- Dictator
- Bottom-line driven
- Makes all decisions
- Some input

Neanderthal

- Total authority
- Power driven
- Dominance
- Makes all decisions
- Scorns input

lines. Quite the contrary. Lean leaders need to learn to lead rather than command. They are more like a quarterback who demands a good deal from his teammates but gives encouragement and praises them when they put out extra effort or make a good play. One thing many need to learn is to understand the distinction between a request and a dictate. Dictates deny an individual's competence. Requests recognize and encourage it. Obviously, requests are always better.

To change a dictate into a request, three things have to happen. The lean leader needs to explain the reason for the command. He or she should actively solicit other opinions. He should ask if the person or group has any questions and willingly answer them.

It's one thing to tell someone to "Turn off the lights" when a presentation is about to start and let it go at that. It's quite another, and much better to say to that person, "Would you please turn off the lights because we're about to start a slide show. And by the way, if you think turning them all off leaves the room too dark, please decide if some should stay on."

Sharing information

Traditionally, managers have used the control of information to maintain their power within their personal fiefdoms, but in the lean enterprise, information is freely shared. Lean leaders understand the more a person knows, the higher the person's sense of ownership of the company and its goals and objectives. This will be discussed at greater length.

Make integrated Decisions

It may sound like something out of "Ripley's Believe It or Not," but some managers hold meetings and make decisions without inviting the people who know the most about a subject. If people are going to have to live with a decision, they ought to have some say in that decision. Otherwise, get ready for undermining to take place. On the other hand, when someone has a hand in a decision, you'd better believe they are going to do their best to make it work. It's best, then, to involve as many people as possible. This doesn't mean a whole crowd of people has to be involved from the get-go. But once the viable options have been identified, it's time to call them in.

Develop People

For people to develop, they need to be treated as though they are capable of correcting their own mistakes. So rather than chastise them when something goes wrong, it will be better to ask them why things didn't go they way they'd hoped, and what they think they might do to change the outcome in the future.

Suppose, for example, a team member really blows a presentation because he or she was not well prepared and was nervous. Rather than read that person the riot act, the lean leader might have a private chat and ask what the person thinks went wrong. Chances are good the team member will say something to the effect that they now realize they weren't sufficiently prepared and got nervous. The lean leader can then ask what the person thinks they might do about that next time. Odds are 99 to one that person will say they need to spend more time preparing, and they need to practice their delivery. Unless this individual is a candidate for a brain transplant, there's little doubt that next time this is what they will do. Our lean leader will have accomplished a great deal more using this approach than the old domineering way would ever have delivered.

Tear Down Barriers

Part of developing people includes removing needless privileges and status symbols that have traditionally separated managers and employees. So say adios to perks like special parking places, company cars, and corporate jets. Everyone should be treated the same. You might also take a look at the dress code. Having one group walking around in pinstripes, pinpoint cotton shirts and club ties, and another in plaid shirts and jeans, doesn't do anything to create a sense of membership on the same team. It does the opposite. And as far as offices go, in many instances, it may actually be beneficial to literally tear down walls so that people are forced to interact. For example, why should a team leader be sitting in an office behind a closed door where no one from his team has easy access to him? He should be with the team, pitching in, with his sleeves rolled up.

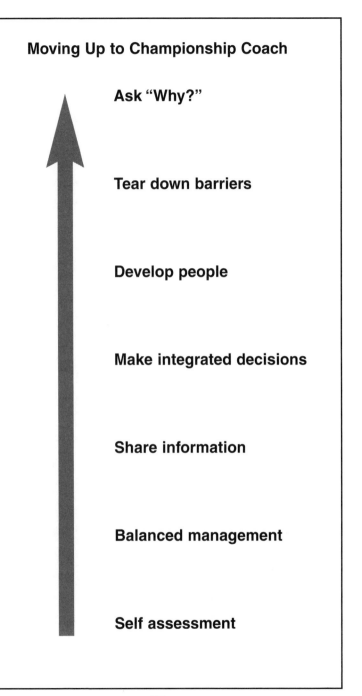

Moving Up to Championship Coach

Ask "Why?"

Tear down barriers

Develop people

Make integrated decisions

Share information

Balanced management

Self assessment

Always Ask "Why?"

Often people do their jobs over and over in the same way, never once asking why something is done one way and not another. Obviously, where there is no curiosity, there will also be no change made for the better. Asking "why?" breaks this cycle and opens the door to innovation in the area of breaking down barriers between managers and employees as well as in situations where there may be a better, easier way to get a job done. I'm reminded of a story told by Jorge Larco and Bruce Henderson in *Lean Transformation.* A woman who was showing her daughter how to cook a leg of lamb. She explained what ingredients were used such as garlic and parsley and other spices. She got out her baking pan, put the leg of lamb on the counter, took a knife, and said, "You begin by cutting the leg here."

She started cutting just above the ankle, and it wasn't easy.

"Why, Mother? Why do you cut the leg?" the daughter asked.

The mother stopped. She looked at the leg. Then her eyes met the daughter's. "To tell the truth, I don't know. It's the way my mother did it."

"Let's give grandma a call," the daughter said.

They soon had her on the line.

"Grandma," the daughter said. "Mom's telling to me how to cook leg of lamb, and I've got a question. Why do you cut the leg?"

"Oh," the grandmother said, and laughed out loud. "Because my pan isn't long enough."

The mother had assumed that cutting the leg was a necessary step. If the daughter hadn't asked why, she and future generations might still be expending energy on an activity that added no value.

Some Thoughts on Leadership

The success of a transformation to lean and the creation of a championship culture will come as a result of the skills, attitudes, and actions of everyone down the line pulling together to move forward. But even though dedication and skill are requisites for success, talented and capable employees aren't all that's needed to win. Something else is equally important. This something is what harnesses the available energy and talent and channels it toward a goal.

Whether it's a sports team, a school class, or a business, for the highest level of effectiveness to be reached, what's needed is solid and consistent leadership. Even a team comprised of outstanding individuals can falter unless a leader gets them working in harmony. You can probably think of a few professional sports teams that have scads of talent but still never seem to make the playoffs.

Much has been written about leadership. In his book, *Billion Dollar Turnaround*, Bill Monahan makes a case that leadership can be boiled down to a single core attribute. Bill is the former Chairman and CEO of Imation Corporation, a company he led from its first dark days when it was struggling and deep in debt all the way to glory as the world leader in digital media storage with plenty of cash and twice the market share of its closest competitor. Bill is without question one of the most dynamic leaders I've met, an opinion apparently shared by his colleagues. Bill believes a leader's personal commitment to the company, the team, or the objective everyone has bought into is what encourages people to follow. Personal commitment compels an individual to take the necessary actions and to have the courage to follow through and persevere until the goal is reached. Personal commitment aligns the thoughts and minds of the leader and the team so that the sum is greater than the parts and even unconscious actions lead toward positive results. And personal commitment breeds the most important ingredient of all, a bond of trust between team members and the leader, trust that the actions to be taken will lead to the best result. Think about it. People may respect another person's intellect but at the same time sense a person is not committed. And like it our not, most people simply are not going to follow someone they don't trust.

Many types of leaders exist, but Bill Monahan would say the trait they all share is commitment to an endeavor, an organization, or a goal. This is needed in order to have the courage and tenacity to continue ahead through tough times. To those around them, such commitment is self evident and leads to the trust among followers written about above. The team knows they can count on their leader to show the way. They are led by example. The leader will reinforce his team's trust by taking responsibility when misfortune occurs.

Giving Credit to Others Builds Loyalty

Rather than take credit for achievements, great leaders build loyalty on top of trust by giving credit where credit is due—and perhaps sometimes even when it is not due. Consider how Ronald Reagan almost never took credit for the achievements of his administration, but instead was quick to praise his staff. In doing so he achieved a very high level of loyalty among his followers.

What else is a great leader able to do? He or she is able to articulate a vision the team can easily grasp. For Reagan it was his "Shining City on a Hill." The leader points the way for the team to proceed to realization of the vision and in doing so generates optimism and bolsters belief the goal can be reached. And, as has been said, "All things are possible to him who believes."

Other Qualities of Great Leaders

Typically, great leaders are good listeners. They want to know what others think, and do not believe they, themselves, always have the best or right answer. They are smart enough to use the intelligence and the experience of others, and understand a good idea can come from anywhere at any time and from anyone. When a great leader comes in contact with an idea that makes sense, he or she recognizes and heeds the sensation of truth that resonates within. You might say the idea or thought seems to "click."

Timid or unsure individuals often will dismiss this feeling. Great leaders are secure with themselves. They see when someone else has a better idea, and they have the self-confidence to put that idea to work.

Great leaders also are demanding. They simply do not tolerate mediocrity. This may be one of the most difficult roles to play because it's human nature to want others to like you, and if you push people hard, they may not like it—or you. Nevertheless, great leaders review and evaluate, and demand improvement and excellence. Jack Welsh at General Electric was reported to be a master at this and had the reputation of constantly having driven his subordinates to the pinnacle of excellence. Vince Lombardi, Winston Churchill, and Louis Gerstner of IBM all used high expectations to achieve goals. They were willing to make the tough decisions and to bring them to reality.

Great leaders have and show respect for the people they lead, whether they are soldiers, employees, players, or citizens. They lead by example and by doing so demonstrate they are worthy of being followed. They are personally committed to the institution they head, as well as the objective of the institution, and are out front personally doing whatever they can to reach it.

Bill Monahan writes about going outside to hire executives who came highly recommended by others in his industry. They had great contacts and used them. They were also very articulate, intelligent, and from all appearances consummate executives. But, once on board, the people who reported to them saw through them. The problem was, they viewed Bill's company, Imation, as a stepping stone to bigger jobs down the road—a way station on a carefully mapped out route. Team members picked up on this and refused to follow them. They knew, perhaps without fully articulating it, who was looking out for number one, and who was committed. This made the road a rough one—the teams questioning the commitment of their leaders.

As Bill wrote, it comes down to what the greatest leader of all time—judging by the number of followers he still has today—said 2000 years ago: "Whoever wants to be great among you must be your servant, and whoever wants to be first must be the slave of all." (Mt 20:26-27) In other words, you don't get to be and stay the leader by serving yourself and having others serve you. People follow because ultimately you are serving them.

Leading by Example

For everyone to pull together for success, executives need to roll up their sleeves and get their hands dirty right next to their employees. They need to be visible and involved, rather than aloof and apart. The goal is for everyone to feel a sense of equality, that they are members of the same team regardless of the title that follows their names. As mentioned, one way to help create this is to eliminate all perks. Like it our not, executives will always be paid more than other employees. It makes sense they should be paid in proportion to the time they must devote, the risks they must take, and the expectations placed on them. But pay is one thing, and perks are another. As has been discussed, it works against a healthy atmosphere to set executives apart, or to place them on a pedestal by giving them perks and other special treatment. That's why, as part of your transformation to lean you need to eliminate executive perks. No fancy offices, no limos, and no exotic meeting locations. Board meetings, for example, need to be held at the company's headquarters or at airport hotels in order to make travel easy and convenient.

Employees are not blind. They see what's going on. They watch the executives closely and determine for themselves if each one is "walking the talk." Let me give you an example, again, from Bill Monahan.

As an early-morning person, he usually found a parking place near the Imation headquarters front door. But one morning he'd been to a breakfast meeting off site and did not get to the lot until mid-morning. All the parking spots in the front lot were taken except those reserved for customers. He drove around, looking, then up the hill to a lot much farther away. Remember, Bill was the Chairman & CEO of a $2.4 billion company. Even so, he walked to the office in ten-degree Fahrenheit weather. He says it was no big deal and thought nothing of it. But during the day two different employees let him know their teams had watched him from their meeting room windows, driving around, looking for a place. They were pleased to see he had not taken a customer spot. Imagine what they would have thought of him if he had.

Face it. Employees quickly figure out which leaders are

personally committed and which are not. They know which ones are only looking out for number one, and they respond to and follow the leaders accordingly. That's why Bill's goal was to create a team at Imation, not stars or prima donnas. That team, led by Bill, not only pulled the company out of debt, Imation's stock price increased 120 percent during the last five years he was there, and the company achieved twice the market share of its closest competitor to become the world leader in removable digital storage media.

Every Manager Won't Make It to Lean Leader

It is a fact that some people will have difficulty with all this. A small percentage of workers and managers will simply be unable or unwilling to change behavior that has become as much a part of them as their hairstyle or the clothes they wear. One year at a "Lean Summit" in Birmingham, England, arranged by Dr. James P. Womack and Professor Daniel T. Jones, I had the opportunity to talk with others who have undergone lean transformation. Almost without exception, "concrete heads" were viewed as the most serious obstacles to progress.

A number of managers at this summit told me if they had it to do over, one thing they definitely would do is get rid of concrete heads quicker. This is something to keep in mind, but you also should know that it is possible to turn some concrete heads around. The question is, how much time should you give them?

The Stages of Adjustment to Change

I'm not a psychologist, but I've been told that predictable stages are passed through when someone deals with a loss or a change in status quo. Stage One is denial, as in, "There's been a mistake. I'm sure I never ran that red light." Yet there is a photo of your model car with your tag number taken by a surveillance camera.

This being the case, when you tell a manager about the changes needed to transform to lean, he or she may think you aren't being serious. He may believe that after a while you'll forget about it and life will go on as always.

Let's say you stick to your guns. Next will be anger.

"The boss can't mean it. I'm valuable to this organization. I can't be forced to do this."

You stick to your guns. Bargaining follows. "Okay, I understand, now. But, some customers aren't going to like it. We're going to have to make some exceptions."

Once more, you hold your ground. The fourth stage is depression. You may notice a change in body language. Slumped shoulders. Dark circles. It's as though the individual was saying, "I've tried to tell them, and they won't listen. No wonder I can't sleep."

Once he or she has reached this stage, you're closer than you think to a conversion. Try to coax this person on to the next stage. "Chin up, and let's get on with it." Once he moves on to the fifth and last stage, which is acceptance, you've got yourself a lean player.

Forewarned is forearmed. In your briefings prior to the start of transformation, it will be helpful to tell managers and workers it's normal to pass through the stages just described, so that they'll understand what's happening. It will not circumvent the process of adjustment, but it will help speed it along.

Personal Transformation will be Required

You will also want to explain that to successfully transform the environment, to become a true lean enterprise, people in the organization must transform as well. This takes serious self-evaluation as has already been pointed out. Seeing ourselves and others in a new light is the first step. It's something we must do, not only in our jobs, but personally. Rather than thinking of ourselves as supervisors or line operators, for example, we must see ourselves as coaches or key players on a team. Rather than regarding others as co-workers or subordinates, we must come to view them as fellow team members.

Let's say a person has done that honest evaluation. With the help of peers, he's identified traits he has that need work. How does he or she go about a personal transformation? How does one reprogram oneself? Some will think this is impossible, of course. "I was born this way. I can't be somebody I'm not," will be their position. They're wrong. Anyone can change, whether losing a hundred pounds is the goal, or changing how we relate to others.

In his book, *The Seven Habits of Highly Effective People,*

Stephen Covey writes about a realization that altered his life. He was wandering among stacks of books in a college library when he came across one that drew his interest. He opened it, and was so moved by what he read that he reread the paragraph many times. It contained the simple idea that a gap exists between stimulus and response, and that the key to growth and happiness is how his gap is used. People have the power to choose in that fraction of a second. If they see a photograph of Boston cream pie, they can choose to order and eat it, or we can decide on raspberry sherbet. Or no dessert at all. If they see a fellow worker who happened to be our subordinate yesterday and who appears to be having difficulty with a particular task, they can direct another worker who also happened to be a subordinate yesterday to help, or they can be the one to help.

Richard Carlson, the author of *Don't Sweat the Small Stuff . . . and It's All Small Stuff,* picks up on the same idea. His advice is always to take a breath before speaking or taking action. If people adopt this, they will rid themselves of the habit of reacting. They will begin taking a considered approach, and taking a considered approach can lead to all sorts of good things such as better relationships with friends, family, and co-workers. It can lead to a slimmer waistline. It can even lead to the transformation from commandant to coach.

Another way is to become what some have called a "silent observer" of yourself. The idea is to move your point of view out of your head, and place it on your shoulder or the ceiling. Then watch yourself go about your business. Once you start keeping an eye out, you may see things that aren't helping you get where you want to go. From here, it's a short step to self transformation. Especially if you take that breath before reacting.

You're Still Going to Have Concrete Heads

Let's say all this has been communicated to workers and managers. Let's say a seminar or training program has been developed and they have taken part in it. Leaders will still need to be prepared to deal with some who simply are not going to make the transformation. More must exist in someone than a passive willingness to change. It takes desire, and some won't have it. Their personal identities may be too closely associated with their jobs. The jailer sees himself as a jailer. He can't picture himself as one of the inmates, even if he gets to be a key player on the inmate soccer team. The commandant views himself as the commandant. Being commandant is what gives him his sense of self worth. He simply will not allow himself to become the coach of the boys in the gulag.

Leaders need to decide in advance how they are going to handle these cases. They must stay alert to the stages, and set a time limit for them to take place. If a worker is not making progress, if it looks as though he or she will never be a team player, perhaps there's a solitary job that still will need doing after the transformation. Leaders need to move him or her into that job quickly and not allow a bad apple to spoil the bunch. The transformation to lean is worth the effort, but never easy. It will be impossible if even a few people are allowed to stand in the way.

Let People Know What to Expect

When the time comes to begin the transformation to lean, management will need to get people together and let them know what is going to happen, and what to expect. A meeting should be held in which plans, objectives, strategies, and the reasons for the transformation are communicated. This is the time to identify the change agent team leaders who will implement the change as well as help the entire group work out organizational and procedural details. The dates of milestones or large group integration meetings ought to be identified. As many questions as possible should be anticipated and answered. Questions should be taken from the floor. The goal is to lay down a road map for the immediate future that will eliminate as much uncertainty as possible during what is sure to be an uncertain time. People should understand why the decision to go lean has been made, that it is essential to remaining competitive, and that it is the only sure way to achieve the company's goals. And they need to know how the transformation will affect them. All the positives as well as negatives should be stated. Their value as workers will be enhanced. They will receive cross training that will make them multi-skilled. They can expect satisfaction with their jobs to increase. They will become empowered. A cleaner, safer working environment will be created. They can expect the company to grow and expand, which will create opportunities which may flow to them.

What marketing research people call "early adapters" and we have called "change agents" will pass through the stages so quickly that you may not see it happen. But it will take time for others, and a few never will. It's likely concrete heads will number about the same as early adapters. But slow pokes need to come around or be out the door for the transformation to take on a life of its own. How much time leadership allows is a judgment call.

They should be firm. Give people time, but not too much.

Recap
- The evolution of leadership is from Neanderthal Despot to Championship Team Coach. This will take time and effort.
- This process can be speeded up by self-assessment, the learning of balanced leadership and how to share information, learning to make integrated decisions, develop people, the tearing down barriers, and always asking, "Why?"
- Leaders must be committed to the organization, its objectives, and the team they lead. People will follow those they sense are fully dedicated to best interest of the team and the greater good of the company. They will not enthusiastically follow those seen as looking out only for number one.
- Giving credit to others builds loyalty.
- True leaders listen and embrace a good idea when they hear one, regardless of its source.
- Leaders lead by example. They do not set

themselves apart from those they lead by accepting or expecting perks or special treatment.

- Not all managers will make the transition to leader because they will be unwilling to let go of behavior they think defines who they are. Others will be able to pass through the first four stages of change to "acceptance" of new ways, although it may take some time.

- A gap exists between stimulus and response during which everyone has the opportunity to choose how they will react.

- Before a lean transformation is begun, everyone who will be affected should be brought up to speed and told what to expect.

Chapter Six: The Mechanics of Change

At least two methods exist for implementing major change. The common approach is called the 'define and convince' model, in which an assigned expert (or expert team) defines the change specifics and convinces the rest of the organization to follow its blueprint. This model works best in small companies, largely because of the close link between the company's leadership and its workers. But in large companies, the process is slow, seldom wins widespread buy-in, and often requires extensive infrastructure and procedural controls to maintain the change.

The other method is the 'participative model.' The leader defines change goals and challenges the work force to define and execute the changes. The actual process involves a series of facilitated large-group sessions for convergence and decision-making, positioned around smaller group activities. This is where the testing and learning takes place. This approach works best because rapid assimilation of knowledge and buy-in usually takes place across the organization. Nevertheless, old line managers often hesitate to use it because it requires the leaders to trust workers, instead of what they perceive as experts with the details.

Participative change roles are quite different from those in the design-and-convince approach. Leaders are not order givers, but participants in learning and decision-making. Experts don't define specific changes, they provide substantive knowledge. Workers are not 'change targets,' but full participants in learning and decision-making.

Even though it is rarely used in manufacturing companies, participative change is not new. I won't go into extensive detail here as there are several books on the subject including *Whole Scale Change* by Dannemiller Tyson Associates and *Large Group Interventions: Engaging the Whole System for Rapid Change* by Barbara Bunker and Billie Alban. These books propose many tools and techniques for engaging the work force. Often they are different in style, but all are based on the idea that the work force should be engaged and involved. Be aware that the approach may benefit from special facilitation skills for orchestrating the large group sessions. Plus, an organization's leader ought to understand the process and have the confidence to empower the work force.

To make change happen, leaders need to set targets and make strategic decisions. The people who have to live with the details make up the group that ought to determine the details. Administrators aren't needed to control the process or define the results. To make sure change happens in a timely fashion, milestones need to be set that will mark key points of system integration. These large group sessions are forums for defining, understanding and decision-making on major integration issues.

Steps of Change

- Top leader consults board of directors (if necessary) and with reports (i.e. primary team), and agreement is reached when and how to implement change.

- If outside counsel is to be used, this is researched and a selection made.

- If downsizing is to occur, positions are researched so they can be combined and the eliminations determined. Exit packages for those who will not continue with the company are decided upon.

- Change agents in each area of the business are selected by the primary team. All functional positions in the new organization are decided upon. Everyone who will remain should be able to see his or her name in a slot when the announcement of the new organization is made.

- First large group meeting is held and entire organization is brought up to speed. Those who will forward with the organization are informed, and those who will not are simultaneously but separately informed. Timetable and milestones are set. All "why" questions are answered. As much uncertainty as possible is eliminated so the company can get on with business.

- Change agents are fully briefed. They select teams from their functional areas in consultation with primary team and meet with them.

- Change agents meet as a cross-functional team to work out direction and to narrow alternatives.

- First milestone meeting is held and consensus reached on initial integration actions.

- Process continues through final milestone meeting and full integration of interlocking teams.

Making Change Happen

System integration points are milestones at which the forced narrowing of possibilities takes place. Directional decisions might be made prior to the large integration meetings in change-agent cross-functional team meetings to winnow down the options. These decisions will be reviewed and the rationale explained at the larger meeting. But to assure buy in, final decisions selected from viable options should be left to the larger group. For this reason, milestone events should be attended by virtually everyone who will continue with the company and be impacted by the change and the new procedures. The more who take part, the better. This is how ownership is achieved. Also, large sessions make the progress highly visible and provide opportunities for visible support by upper management. This is important to maintaining momentum.

Change Decision Making

In traditional businesses, decisions for a new system are typically made by a few experts, and they are handed down from the top. But in the method suggested here, most change decisions are made at the integrating sessions with the help of facilitators trained in gaining consensus. Things should run smoothly if alternatives are worked out ahead of time by smaller groups who represent the whole, headed by leaders who have the respect of others.

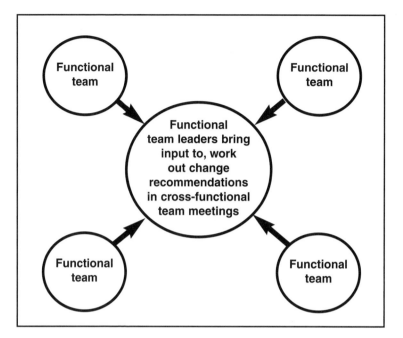

Recap

- At least two methods exist for implementing change. The best for becoming a lean enterprise is the participative model in which the entire organization participates so all can have input. This assures buy in.
- Those who will have to live with the details and procedures of the new organization should decide what they are. Then the obligation will be on them to make them work, or to change the procedures.
- Change agents chosen by the primary team will form teams to recommend change options. Details are worked out and narrowed down by cross-functional team made up of the leader of each functional team.
- Milestones for steps to take place in the process should be set by the primary team. To the extent possible, the full organization will be present at these meetings and select from viable options.

Chapter Seven: How to Make Teams Work

People who aren't used to working on teams and leading teams are going to need some help getting up to speed. That's what this chapter is about.

Anyone who has read this far knows a basic tenet of the lean enterprise is to push decision making to those personnel closest to a situation. Who can possibly be in a better position to recognize what needs to be done in a given situation than someone who is right there on the spot? This is done through empowered teams of which there are two types: home teams and cross-functional teams comprised of individuals from various disciplines, whose job it is to address specific tasks or assignments. All teams are "empowered" because they can, within defined boundaries, decide on the best course of action and take it. Individuals must shift from a mind set where supervisors told them what to do to one where the group makes decisions on such things as who will work overtime, who will fill in for a worker who is out sick, and what can be done to boost output to meet a looming deadline. Team members will have to think outside of the box in order to determine how processes can be improved and what changes should be implemented. Perhaps as important, teams can help build an atmosphere of cooperation and esprit d'corps. For teams to function properly, though, people must learn how to be team players. It will help if they have advance knowledge concerning what to expect when individuals are brought together into a unit with specific goals and objectives.

The Stages of Team Growth

Teams typically progress through four stages. Recognizing these and anticipating the challenges likely to to be faced will help ensure smooth growth and ultimate success. Stage one is called "Forming." It is marked by uncertainty and distance between members. People in the group feel unsure about their roles and relationships. You might think of it as the "becoming acquainted" part of a team's life cycle. The next stage, which is called "Norming," occurs when the team begins to settle down to become an efficient unit. Predictable patterns emerge and a style of work develops. "Storming," which happens next, is what transpires when conflicts arise. This is the critical stage, so leaders need to manage the situation and persevere. Some teams don't survive. Members may want to fold up the tent and throw in the towel rather than continue. But the team should be encouraged to get on with it and iron out the problems. Let them know that "Storming" is normal, that it's a necessary stage and the prelude to a productive stage that comes next. This final and fruitful stage is "Performing," when a mature team can be counted on to deliver solutions. "Performing" often is at its most spectacular in high-pressure situations, on tight deadlines, or under conditions that may require super-human effort. Top performing teams can create amazing results. Consider, for example, the team that worked to bring

---

Stages of Team Growth

1. Norming—becoming acquainted

2. Forming—"getting to know you"

3. Storming—staking territory

4. Performing—finding solutions.

---

back safely the crew of the crippled Apollo 13 spacecraft on its ill-fated mission to the moon.

Teamwork can result in an extraordinary experience that members will never forget. The bonding that results can be very strong. Even in the case of groups with modest missions, teamwork can replace apathy and discouragement with pride and enthusiasm. At the very least, members of a team that has passed through the stages we've mentioned must have learned to listen sincerely and to speak the truth, as opposed to venting and bellyaching. Caring about the success of the team and about teammates is half the battle. This can go a long way toward helping people learn how to put what may be good for the group as a whole ahead of selfish motives.

A team can be almost any group that has closely linked jobs, and can cut across what would be different departments in a traditional organization. To break down the barriers in a cross-functional team, it helps to think of team members as representatives of various disciplines rather than as having different functions. The distinction is subtle, but it helps bring down walls.

Every effort should be made to keep teams consistent from one day to the next. Individuals should remain together as much as possible so that esprit d'corps can build and the "performing" stage can be reached and maintained.

Choosing a Team Leader

Working through teams rather than the typical hierarchy fosters a sense of equality, but this doesn't mean leaders aren't important or necessary. That's why team leaders need to be appointed by the primary team rather than elected by the team they lead. Appointment confers approval from the top for the leader to network across the organization. A team leader's role, particularly the leader of a cross-functional team, is to bring together a diverse and sometimes skeptical group for a common purpose, to ensure the team operates effectively, and to manage a team project that crosses what are typically boundaries in traditional organizations. A team leader should understand the impact of change, support meaningful change aligned with organizational objectives, help create an environment for learning, and employ tools and techniques that will provide direction and measure progress for team-based decision-making. This is why criteria for appointment of a team leader should include:

- *A stake in the team's mission.* The leader should identify with the team's objectives. If, for example, the development of a new soft drink involves production, marketing, and sales, the marketing representative who encouraged new product development may be the logical choice.

- *Technical competence.* The leader should be recognized as good at whatever she or he does. This inspires trust during team formation. If a marketer is known to have developed effective campaigns for well-known brands, he or she may have more initial credibility with the new team—even if team leadership is a new role.

- *Interpersonal skills.* The leader should have knowledge of communication systems, team formation, decision-making, and conflict resolution. He or she should have a track record of inspiring trust and cooperation.

- *Project management skills.* The leader should know how to deploy resources, organize work, and focus on outcomes.

- *Adaptability and flexibility.* The leader should recognize change as opportunity, and be able to modify plans to meet changes in the work environment.

- *A spirit of service.* The leader should want the job in order to make this contribution.

Choosing Team Members

In the case of cross-functional teams, it's usually best if team members are chosen by the appointed team leader. Giving the leader the authority to choose the team, which is best done in consultation with other leaders who will have a stake in the outcome of team's work, will heighten his or her sense of responsibility and accountability about getting the task done. Even so, care should be taken to make sure a team has all the members it needs. What follows is a story that demonstrates why.

A team was formed in response to a reader survey that had evaluated a newspaper's entertainment section. The paper was one of several competing in a large metropolitan area. The team included representatives from editorial, production, and distribution. No one from advertising sales was asked to participate.

The team decided to integrate national entertainment news with local arts events, plays and concerts. What looked to be a lively and dynamic new section was created. But after a few months the team was reconvened. The problem was minimal advertising support.

This time, the team pulled in a representative from ad sales. Prospective advertisers for the section were surveyed and the problem identified. The new section was in a tabloid format, which uses full newspaper pages turned on their sides and folded to make a dimensionally smaller section than the rest of the paper. Since there was more than one newspaper serving the area, this required advertisers to design specific ads to fit this section, or to rescale existing ads that had been created to run on full-size pages. Many of the advertisers surveyed did not want to go to this additional trouble and expense.

The section's design was changed to a full-size format

and immediately it began attracting more advertising space. If the team had included a representative from advertising sales in the first place, it might have avoided unnecessary rework and loss of revenue during the quarter the new section ran in tabloid format.

Diversity Prevents Myopia

This leads to another important point, which is the value of diversity on cross-functional teams. This is not just about only race, gender, age or sexual orientation. To come up with innovative solutions, diversity of *thought* is as important as other differences. This includes extroverts and introverts, R&D's viewpoint, as well as sales and marketing flash and glitter. It's important to avoid picking people with one style only, or a team can end up with everyone who thinks the same, in which case alternative but effective approaches are likely to be missed. Respecting peoples' differences leads to positive interaction, as well as the ability to listen to and consider creative options.

According to the Myers-Briggs system for categorizing personalities, there are sixteen basic types. Imagine how myopic a team would be if all its leaders had the same one. Yet this can easily happen.

The fact is, unless cautioned to do otherwise, it is human nature for leaders to pick team members who resemble themselves in terms of personality type. The old saying "birds of a feather flock together" is true. If a person is what some would call a "born leader," an ENFJ in the

Meyers-Briggs system, he will probably look for others who share preferences for objective decision making as well as structure, precise scheduling, and order. But don't be mistaken. Those who don't share these traits can be equally competent, but in a system driven by profits and productivity, those who possess these preferences have the edge. This is not to say those who make decisions based on how something makes them *feel*—as opposed to strict logic—cannot cut it in the management world. Many do. In fact, according to authorities on this subject, all sixteen types can be found in management positions of major corporations and government agencies. Still, the overwhelming majority fall into "Thinking and Judging" (TJ) category as opposed to "Intuitive-Feeling" (IF). Yet having people around who bring a different perspective to things is extremely beneficial to out-flanking the competition.

A team of all ENTJs (Extroverted, Intuitive, Thinking, Judging) will view the world in largely black-and-white terms. Things will be either right or wrong. When two of them disagree, one sees black and the other sees white. In this case, there will be few alternative solutions short of pulling rank and status, shouting more loudly, or becoming increasingly more stubborn. Sometimes the source of the disagreement can become obscured and one may have to ask, are the parties disagreeing with the matter at hand, or are they reacting to the fact that they can see themselves in each other? Often it's hard to tell. In the end, productivity becomes curtailed.

Contrast this to a team with a broader mix of types.

Studies show that diversity engenders creativity. The more diversity of personnel on any given task, the better the final product will be, if differences are respected, authenticated, and integrated; and communication remains open. Clearly, with many different points of view, projects may take longer to accomplish, but the end result will have more people committed to it because more people had a chance to influence the process, and there will be a greater sense of pride. Also, a strong leader will have the opportunity to listen to all points of view, then to choose and move aggressively and quickly.

At one time or another most managers have been through the management training exercise in which they are lost at sea—or in a desert or on the moon—as the result of a crash. All that's left are a handful of specific items, ranging from a case of scotch to a small mirror to a piece of cheese. The task they're given is to rank-order the items in terms of their importance to survival.

In this exercise each manager must independently come up with his or her own rank order. Then groups of managers are assigned to arrive at some consensus of the ranking. This process parallels real-life group decision making—people arrive at the meeting with some opinions, a little knowledge, and must react to the people with whom they work to reach a group decision.

The final scores in this training exercise are usually set against some "expert" criteria. Repeatedly, groups that have the widest diversity of knowledge, a group ranging for example from a former Marine who's an expert in desert survival to an accountant who's never spent a night under the stars, will come up with the list most closely aligned to the "correct" answers—provided the group respects their diversity and communicates openly about differences of opinion.

Changing from Manager to Leader

Suppose someone who was a supervisor now is team leader of the same group of individuals. The question is often raised, "What can be done or said to get the supervisor to shift gears and become a coach?"

Two things. One is a stick, the other a carrot. First, his home team leader can make it clear the individual has a choice of either changing, or leaving. The carrot is a "job well done." Improved performance and goals accomplished must now provide the rewards that motivate the former supervisor, rather than the feeling of being in a position of power over others. This will work if the focus can be shifted where it belongs—to end results—to filling customer needs, to increased quality, and lower costs.

Frequency of Meetings

Manufacturing plants that perform best have meetings between operators and leaders at the beginning of each shift. Offices of workers in service industries can do the same. These meetings last 10-15 minutes. The group looks at its performance from the day before, and at production goals for the day ahead. Work assignments are reviewed and any special instructions noted. Quality or production issues are reviewed. If someone on the team didn't come to work, or if someone has to leave early, this will be discussed and how to handle it resolved. Overtime schedules are reviewed and replacements determined if necessary. Whether the group is ahead or behind its production schedule is discussed. If it is behind, the group decides what can be done to catch up.

Once a week, groups also meet for half an hour to discuss performance issues. This is the forum for suggestions on how to improve. If suggestions made in previous meetings haven't been implemented, a report is made on where they stand.

Add up the time spent in meetings and you'll find that workers spend an hour and a half each week, which may seem excessive. But it pays. In one plant, unit output ranged from 42,000 to 45,000 product units each day prior to the implementation of daily and weekly meetings. Today, the same plant averages 54,000 units a day with no increase in the number of people. And that's not all. The plant had been producing 2,000 boxes a day, and 120 to 150 of these were rejected largely due to quality problems. Now the same plant produces 2,400 boxes a day and no boxes are rejected. Zero. Rework has been substantially reduced and virtually eliminated.

When a quality problem arises in this plant, the operators involved are sent to call on the customer. Imagine what happens when a team member who has heard about a problem firsthand gets together the next day with the rest of the team. The impact is dramatic. People pay attention. Problems are taken seriously, and solutions are quickly found. This is continuous pursuit of improvement in action.

Celebrate Successes

In the transition to team empowerment, it is important to celebrate successes. Most leaders are quick to have a meeting to talk about what isn't going right. They are correct in doing so. But in order to provide positive reinforcement, meetings also should be held about what is going right. There should be celebrations. The head of manufacturing or the general manager might buy coffee for the team that has scored a success. Everyone who had a hand in the success should be invited—but only those who had a hand. Allowing interlopers to join in can destroy the meaning, and water down the significance of the celebration. Let the others score their own successes, and get their own coffee and donuts and a pat on the back.

Bringing Down Walls

Empowered teams are a fundamental way of working throughout the lean enterprise. In a figurative sense, they help bring down walls between departments, but I've seen that it can actually help to literally bring them down. It's best to strive for as much transparency as possible by putting everyone together where they can see one another and are encouraged to interact. For example, in many large organizations, process and design engineers do not speak to one another unless absolutely necessary, even though they are in the same building. Design Engineering develops the product and then "slips the blueprints under the door." If this is the case in your organization you might put all engineers on one floor with no walls whatsoever. In any case, many problems can be eliminated before they occur if design engineers are required to present their design to other disciplines, such as process engineering and marketing and sales, in a design review meeting at various stages in the development process. The design engineers should then consider all suggestions and report back to the group concerning the modifications made.

Product Design Teams

Teams such as these should be comprised of representatives of all areas of the business that have a stake in a product, including sales, marketing, and the customer. A customer representative can add a great deal to such a team, insuring the end product will be right on target and accepted. In our lean advertising development process, we involve our clients early on to help us narrow down the possible directions so that we can focus on fleshing out one or two. Typically, ad agencies do the winnowing themselves and show the client only what in their opinion is the best direction. Clients often reject the approach they've selected and ask to see more options. By building in a checkpoint with the client early on, we have eliminated a good deal of the wheel spinning agencies typically endure.

In addition to client representation, the team should also have representatives from finance and materials supply because the end product will benefit from the perspective of each. Products should be designed for ease of manufacturing, and this requires a clear understanding of the manufacturing process. It makes sense, therefore, for process engineering to have a seat on the team.

The Role of Human Resources

As the organization evolves, the role of Human Resources will become increasingly important. The head of the company needs to define the culture to be attained, and Human Resources must identify changes that have to be accomplished in order to arrive at this. Human Resources also should remain attentive to developments that may throw up impediments to a lean enterprise culture. This means having a steady finger on the pulse of the company grapevine, and advising the various leaders on activities to be performed in order to ensure a successful cultural change. The transformation no doubt will require consistent and systematic training of everyone in the company.

Rules Are Still Needed

Teams are empowered but this doesn't mean there are no rules. It's important people know their boundaries.

Perhaps you have heard or read about something that took place at an elementary school that illustrates this. The school was located in a open area without many trees so it was possible to see a long way. The playground behind the school had no fence. Practically all of the children stayed within twenty feet or so of the school building, apparently afraid to venture very far. The school's principal had a fence built around the playground, and once it was up, the children dispersed themselves evenly throughout the fenced-in area.

Without clear boundaries the children had felt insecure and had stayed close to the building where they felt safe.

So, too, it is with teams. Knowing the boundaries sets people free to operate within those boundaries, and this can lead to higher productivity than would be the case if no boundaries existed.

The boundaries, or rules should include:

1. Everyone is on a home team. Membership isn't optional.

2. Every home team must have a minimum of one weekly business-focused, action-driven meeting. Cross-functional teams should meet as frequently as necessary for deadlines to be met.

3. Everyone must be on time to meetings.

4. Every team must report to the primary team (top team in the organization) concerning decisions made, actions to be taken, who is to take them and deadlines which have been agreed upon. (Action reports, which will be explained shortly, are the mechanism for this.)

5. Each team must keep a notebook that includes current action reports, an up-to-date objectives sheet, (also explained below) and other pertinent information. This will be a "public record" anyone within the organization can access in order to find out the status of any of the team's action items, or to get up to speed on where the team stands. The notebook should always be complete and up-to-date, allowing anyone to step in and keep things moving in the leader's absence.

6. Decisions that affect other areas of the business should be made only by a cross-functional team that includes representatives from all the areas that will be affected.

RULES, ALSO known as "non-negotiables," establish minimum standards for performance and behavior. They give leaders a framework to give their organizations habit, discipline and structure. These in turn create and sustain a sense of urgency, a clear and concise business focus, and drive a sense of collective accountability.

Using Action Reports

Action reports are a device many advertising agencies use to make sure work gets done for clients. In ad agencies I worked for and ran, very little would have gotten done and a great deal of important stuff would have fallen through the cracks without them. Every member of the team who worked on a client's business got a copy of a

Lean Enterprise Ground Rules

- Everyone must be on a home team.

- Home teams must meet once a week at minimum.

- Everyone must be on time.

- All teams must report to the primary team on decisions, actions, and deadlines.

- If a deadline cannot be met, a new deadline must be negotiated with the team leader prior to the next team meeting.

- Each team must keep a notebook up-to-date which is a public record to include action reports, objectives sheet, team rules, regulations and bylaws.

- The team is empowered to make decisions affecting its functional area.

- Decisions that affect other areas must be made by a cross-functional team including representatives from all affected areas.

report when it was issued, as did the the agency's contact at the client company. That the client saw this report is comparable to a home team sending a report to the primary team of its organization. This needs to be one of the non-negotiables. Having the action report for review serves a check. If something seems in error, or off base, it's incumbent upon the client, or the primary team, to question it. Plus, that the primary team has been alerted certain actions will be taken put the onus to follow through on those who are to take the action.

An action report is similar to the minutes of a meeting except it leaves out superfluous discussion and zeros in on decisions made and actions to be taken. It states specifically the individual who is to take action on each item, and the deadline agreed upon.

Action Reports Make People Accountable

It's one thing to tell a team member he or she is accountable for an action. It's another for him to take this seriously. With action reports, accountability is in black and white. Nothing could be clearer because it's right there on paper. And because no question about accountability can possibly exist, team leaders no longer must rely only on those they feel they can depend on. After all, everyone will be looking, including the people who run the business since the report goes to the primary team. How an individual performs in terms of completing actions on time relative to his peers will be a major factor in his or her performance reviews. These means everyone in the organization will be obliged to pull his or her own weight or face the inevitable consequences.

Action Reports Increase Meeting Effectiveness

Action reports contribute to team meeting effectiveness because they document action items that result from team meetings. Because individual accountability is identified, there can be no misunderstanding about who was supposed to do what. Meetings begin with a review of items that should have been completed, and conclude with a review of new action items identified during the meeting, verification of who is responsible for each action, and agreement on target completion dates. If someone doesn't think he can get a particular item completed in the allotted time, that person needs to say so, and why. Then a different date can be negotiated and agreed upon. Also, if something unforeseen comes up between meetings and an item is not going to be completed by the agree-upon date, the team member needs to see the leader about it prior to the next meeting and establish a new date. This needs to be a team rule, or "non-negotiable."

Action Reports Are Invaluable at Review Time

Action reports help leaders gauge performance. When leaders counsel with team members—including formal appraisals—they have documentation of performance in hand. They can quickly identify the number and significance of actions an employee has taken and whether or not he or she consistently makes target completion dates. This allows leaders to be specific and constructive in developing performance.

Action Reports Build Trust

Action reports build trust between leaders, team members and top management. They eliminate the need for finger-pointing and establish responsibility that can't be questioned. The result is that individuals learn to trust each other to live up to their commitments. The primary team can and should review these reports and acknowledge teams that are contributing in important ways to the performance of the business.

Here are some tips to use action reports effectively:

1. Be specific. Each action item must be detailed enough so that anyone reviewing the register a year from now will understand it.

2. Always designate one person who is ultimately accountable. Sometimes several individuals are involved in an action. List all the names, but specify the person who has to make it happen.

3. Use specific dates, never ASAP or other acronyms. These mean different things to different people. As soon as possible may mean by the end of the day to one team member and by the end of next week to another.

4. Keep a record of renegotiated dates. Records need to

Action Report United Manufacturing

Action to be taken	Responsible	Deadline	Date completed	Comments

be kept in such a way anyone can easily see a history and trends. This is important information that may have significance in performance reviews.

5. Record and indicate the exact completion date. This clearly documents when the action was completed and shows which team members consistently get the job done within their committed times.

6. Renegotiate a new target completion date prior to due date. Team members must be made aware that if conditions change, and they cannot complete the task by the due date, it's their responsibility to bring it to the leader's attention and renegotiate a new date prior to the upcoming meeting. This is critical so that team members with actions contingent upon those of that particular individual can modify their target completion dates accordingly.

7. Archive action reports. They can be maintained electronically, or as hard copies, but an up-to-date hardcopy should always be placed in the team notebook where everyone has access to it.

8. Don't assign an action to someone who is absent from a meeting. An individual ought not be held accountable for completing an action he had no say in accepting.

Communication is Critical

In employee surveys, one complaint that employees consistently make is a "lack of communication." Most organizations respond by putting in place more programs that focus on sharing information and data: newsletters, videos, electronic boards, town-hall meetings and similar things. These programs may have a place, but they are not communication. And they aren't what employees want.

Employees want to hear and to be heard. They want information—but they want to be able to look their leaders in the eye when it is given to them. They want the opportunity to give their opinions and to ask questions. The only way to do that effectively is face-to-face.

Communication is the delivering and receiving of information in a personal, two-way manner. It occurs with the exchange of words that convey meaning, as well as through intonation and body language.

All the other ways of exchanging information are advertising—a one-way method of sharing information that does not assure effective internalization. Advertising has its place, to be sure. Once two-way communication has taken place, the information can be reinforced through various advertising means, such as e-mail, bulletin boards, company newsletters and electronic messaging boards.

No matter how well or graphically sophisticated the delivery, however, advertising is just advertising. It can never take the place of face-to-face exchange—and that's coming from an old ad guy.

The primary team should define the non-negotiables of organizational communication. For communication to become ingrained in the organization, it must be disciplined, routine, structured and involve everyone in the organization.

Making Communication Happen

Communication is a two-way street. And in a successful organization, communication is not a random event. It is a planned process, just like any business function.

When leaders plan communication strategy, they ought to incorporate these key elements to focus meetings to action, (not endless discussion), enable participation, and provide a consistent flow of information throughout the organization.

• *Minimum frequency.* Since the primary two-way communication vehicle is the home-team meeting, the primary (top) team needs to establish the minimum frequency standard, based on business cycles and needs. All teams must meet at this minimum frequency to ensure timely communication around the business.

• *Purpose and outcomes.* Define in advance the business purpose and outcomes you desired from meetings. Specifying the purpose and outcomes of meetings enables focused preparation and clarity around topics and defines the level of urgency for activities that result from the meeting.

• *Agenda.* Plan meetings around an agenda, which not only lists the topics to be discussed, but also the time frames in which to discuss them and the person who will lead the discussion/presentation. A structured agenda forces the focus onto important business matters and helps create a sense of urgency.

• *Preparation.* Determine in advance how the communication should occur. What information needs to be passed up and down to all home teams and by when? What information needs to be brought into the meeting from other home teams? The agenda ought to include a status update of outstanding actions from the previous meeting as well as a verification of new actions that arise during the meeting so there is absolute clarity about who is doing what and when.

• *Roles and responsibilities.* Meetings need a leader, a recording secretary and a time keeper. These roles must be identified and filled prior to the meeting so that individuals come prepared to fulfill them. Filling these roles ensures someone is ready to facilitate the agenda, document actions, capture pass-up/pass-down information and document decision and key discussion points.

• *Rotation plan.* For routine, standard meetings a rotation plan for filling these roles among participants ensures that meetings are governed by process and are not dependent on the personalities of different individuals.

Recap
- Teams typically pass through several stages of growth: forming, norming, storming and performing.
- A team leader should be chosen by the primary team in order to lend authority and credibility to that leader.
- Members of cross-functional teams should be

selected by the appointed leader in consultation with those who have a stake in the team's work, thus putting the onus on the team leader for a successful outcome.

- Care should be taken to insure members are chosen who have a diversity of personalities so that "group think" is avoided.
- Each area of the business that will be affected by a team's work should be represented so that important aspects are not overlooked.
- Successes should be celebrated. Interlopers should not be allowed at these celebrations.
- Literally bringing down walls is one way to force people to interact.
- Teams need rules or non-negotiables in order operate freely within clear boundaries.
- A team's business should be organized in a notebook that becomes a public record of it's work.
- Action reports that assign responsibility for actions and completion dates should be distributed to every member of a team and to the primary team of an organization. They force accountability and are valuable for use in performance reviews.
- For communication to be effective it must be frequent and face-to-face. Emails and memos fall into the category of advertising.

Chapter Eight: Creating Urgency

One job of the primary or top team of an organization should be to set overall goals to be accomplished during the year or the quarter. In a manufacturing business transforming to lean, these might include goals to do with inventory turns, throughput, customer PPM, on-time delivery, and a host of other metrics. In the ever-more competitive global economy in which most companies now operate, a business must continue to improve and become more competitive or risk extinction. In a traditional organization, the top executive typically hands out objectives to his various reports who assign them down the line. In the case of the lean enterprise, the primary or top team determines the objectives and divvies them out to various home and cross-functional teams. The individual teams determine how they will meet these objectives.

You might ask how the primary team can be sure progress is being made? And, what can each team and the primary team do to monitor progress? I suggest a mechanism we will label the "objectives worksheet," which is a simple and concise tracking mechanism that will allow the team to monitor and respond to key business metrics. Its purpose is to provide a clear focus for each team and to establish accountability for each team's expected contributions. It will also serve to create a sense of urgency.

Every team should have an objectives worksheet. The

primary team should design it using a standard format so that it is consistent throughout the organization in order to eliminate the possibility of confusion or misunderstanding.

The primary team ought to begin by working out a global worksheet, which will measure overall organizational performance. The global worksheet's specific objectives will be high-level. The objectives incorporated on worksheets at other organizational levels should combine to support these overall objectives. The primary team should review the global worksheet weekly at its team meeting. The rest of the organization should be privy to the global worksheet, too, and be kept abreast of progress toward global objectives perhaps monthly during one of their home-team meetings. This will not only keep everyone in the company informed on progress, it will create peer pressure throughout the organization to make the numbers since everyone will be working toward these goals.

This openness may go against the grain of some traditional managers. We've all seen those who guarded information. They may even have kept it under lock and key. After all, information is power. Their line of thinking must go something like this: *If I have it and you don't, that makes me more powerful than you. If I'm more powerful, that makes me superior, doesn't it?*

If employees don't know how the company is doing, if they don't even know how *they* are doing, how can they be expected to improve?

This is one reason top-level lean leaders make sure everyone in the enterprise knows the size of the company,

Objectives Worksheet United Manufacturing

Item	Objective	Plan/Strategy to meet	Owner	January	February
Throughput					
				Comments	Comments
On time delivery					
				Comments	Comments
Quality/ppm					
				Comments	Comments
Safety					
				Comments	Comments

the sales, and key financial indicators. But it is not the only reason. You'll recall that a sense of belonging, an esprit d'corps, is part of what enables an organization to get ahead and stay ahead of the competition. It's pretty difficult to be proud of what you are, and how you are doing, if you don't know what you are and how you are doing.

Readily available information, information that can be had for the asking, is not all that's being talked about here. Leaders need to be sure people know what's happening day by day and even hour by hour in a manufacturing plant. People should start each day with a brief meeting to review the prior day's performance and to establish goals for the day ahead. Information about how the day is going should be posted as frequently as every hour on boards or monitors everyone can see. These postings might track through-put of work cells, quality performance, cost and delivery performance, corrective maintenance and machine performance, as well as the training status of individuals, and other team measurements.

The lean factory is a "visual" factory. Leaders in service businesses would do well to consider how some of the techniques used might be adapted to their situation. Production line scoreboards keep an assembly team appraised of hourly production. All around the factory, walls display charts and graphs—which are frequently updated—keep everyone informed about such things as output compared to goals, sales and profit year-to-date, quality levels, inventory turns, training schedules and the progress made by individuals who are in training. The list of what is tracked reflects what's important for a particular business and group of people.

A visual factory doesn't stop at metrics. Instructions for performing procedures are displayed where they are needed, and there are pictorials employing drawings, diagrams, and schematics, rather than written words, which may not be as easily understood.

Kanbans (cards, signs or other means of conveying information) are used to identify arriving inventory and are sent along with empty containers to signal the stock room or a supplier that the time has come to replenish an item. Kanbans accompany products sent to customers, who eventually will return them to signal a reorder. With all this information readily available, it should be possible to judge a production cell's performance from a quick look around.

In short, in the lean enterprise information is in the open for all to see and use, rather than buried in a computer or locked in a manager's desk.

Supporting the Company's Overall Objectives

Once the company objectives worksheet is complete, teams ought to begin to develop worksheets specifically defining how they support the organization's goals. Ideally, each team should have at least one objective for each key area that's been targeted for improvement.

Worksheet development cascades throughout all levels until every team in the organization has a worksheet with specific metrics that reflect the team's area of responsibility.

A team's objectives worksheet should be is reviewed at all its meetings as a standing agenda item. A quick look at progress toward objectives will quickly set the tone of a meeting. Reviewing and discussing worksheets lends a sense of urgency to home team-meetings, particularly when an area may be falling behind. During discussion, the team should identify what appears to be working, and for performance that's below target, develop corrective action plans.

Worksheets also identify who owns responsibility for tracking progress toward a particular objective and for keeping others focused on it. Of course, the objective owner is not responsible for accomplishing the objective all by himself, but he is responsible for updating the worksheet prior to each meeting and for making sure it is accurate.

Another way a sense of urgency is created is that teams must share worksheets with the primary, senior leadership team. Typically, each home team sends its worksheet with corresponding corrective action plans to the primary team monthly for review. Many organizations go a step farther and replace this with monthly presentations to senior leaders. The leader of each home team must report on progress being made toward objectives. Responsibility for this presentation can also be rotated among team members monthly, thus creating even more urgency.

A worksheet or presentation clearly demonstrating how a team is contributing to the business makes a very powerful statement and can be highly motivating to the team that presents it—as well as to other teams which then become challenged to do as well.

Training May Be Needed

Organizing the work force into teams requires people to learn how to function as a team and to take on the various roles required. Companies can ensure team process goes smoothly by sponsoring training sessions to develop team skills. Teams need to develop at their own pace and to adjust according to their own problem-solving skills and resources.

You might:

I. Develop a company wide team training program focusing on the fundamentals needed in good teamwork, such as interpersonal skills, clearly defined roles and responsibilities, brainstorming, problem solving techniques.

2. Create a way to evaluate and measure teamwork. The team notebook can be an excellent tool in this regard.

3. After creating the teams, focus on implementing team structure to help teams take on their new responsibilities.

Here's a checklist:
- Define responsibilities.
- Categorize responsibilities into similar functions.
- Give each category a position and name.
- Ask team members to volunteer to fill each position.
- Rotate positions among members for different lengths of time, depending on the complexity of the

assignment. This will maximize knowledge and experience.

• Make sure every team member fills each position at least once.

Work Flows Toward Competence

Managing by personality is one of the pitfalls some fall into as a result of downsizing and moving to empowered teams. All the touchy-feely leadership stuff of the last decade has not served well those who need to lead others in business. Dictating can be counterproductive, too, of course, just as touchy-feeling is not the way to get an organization moving ahead like a well-oiled machine. The use of objectives worksheets and action reports will solve this. The system outlined here using worksheets and action reports can insure leaders don't subconsciously play favorites. It forces everyone to accept accountability. Each person must pull his or her own weight or be exposed to peers. And, as any parent of a teenager knows, peer pressure can be powerful. One thing is certain. Team leaders can end up doing all the team's work if they don't have a such system in place.

Establishing non-negotiables is step number one. Once these clear ground rules are laid, a leader can get things going in a hurry. He or she needs to remember to communication face-to-face. People need to know what's going on and putting it in an e-mail or memo simply won't do. Next is an auditable system or process using action reports and worksheets to create accountability and urgency.

All this sounds like it should work, but what happens if a leader has a problem employee who just doesn't seem to get it, keeps making excuses, or tries to put responsibility on the team leader for a problem he or she should solve? It's time for some face-to-face communication:

1. *Identify and discuss the issues.* When an employee brings the leader a problem, the two should discuss it and identify who should solve it. Most problems don't need the leader's intervention. People can solve problems themselves, provided they have the tools to do so.

2. *Assign the responsibility.* Record it on the action report register. If the employee can solve the problem, make the employee responsible for it. Of course, make sure she has the knowledge and resources. If she doesn't, clearly define what she needs to do. The leader can take responsibility for tasks the team member doesn't have the resources to accomplish. For example, the leader might help on those the member doesn't have the knowledge to complete. In the process, the leader should teach the employee how so he or she can do it without help the next time.

3. *The leader needs to follow up.* When she does, she will find one of three things:

• The employee carried out his responsibility and solved the problem. Nothing more is required.

• The employee has run into some problems. She needs the leader's help to remove barriers. For example, she needs the leader's signature to authorize her to purchase supplies. The leader needs to give that support and establish a new follow-up time to make sure the employee followed through.

• The employee did nothing. This is where most leaders drop the ball. If a leader lets the employee do nothing, he has encouraged behavior that cannot be tolerated. If the employee does nothing, he should receive a new deadline and be reminded that his inaction will be reflected in his next performance review.

FOLLOWING THROUGH is the hardest part in getting employees trained in completing actions. Leaders should not let anyone off the hook. They need to remember, a leader's job is not to solve all of a team member's problems. Their job is to enable team members to solve their own problems. This is true empowerment.

But frankly, I don't think non-compliance will last very long or happen very frequently if the new system is implemented and followed faithfully because I know the system works.

How I Learned This System and That It Works

As an relatively young executive in advertising who had just moved from Baltimore to Richmond, I decided to join the local chapter of the American Marketing Association. I did so for the same reason others join clubs made up of people in the business they're in. I wanted to network and get to know others in order to make a name for myself and to attract business to my firm.

After a year or so, I ran for office and was elected vice president of programming, the guy who had to line up the monthly speakers. There were five or six vice presidents of this club, each with a different area such as membership, fund raising, and special events. The way things got done was through meetings of the officers which were called "directors' meetings." To keep this meetings running in an orderly fashion, Robert's Rules of Order was followed. At first I thought these Rules were kind of silly, but it wasn't long before I saw how they served a purpose. They assured orderly procedures were followed, and they resulted in consistency. A notebook was kept of all the minutes of every meeting. This notebook also held pertinent information concerning what each vice president did during the year such as a list of contact information for suppliers, and copies of invoices for items that had been purchased. This made a lot of sense. Every year the membership of the American Marketing Association changed somewhat. And every year the list of officers turned over, and a new president took the reins. People found themselves filling roles they knew very little about. But the club's purpose and direction and momentum continued because that notebook contained the information they needed to pick up where others had left off. In addition to the Rules of Order, the AMA also had a charter, bylaws, and written procedures. Without these, when new officers assumed their positions, it might have taken practically the whole year for them to get a handle on things.

At each meeting, the secretary kept minutes. These minutes served as a history and also helped keep everyone on their toes, because they were a public record of what the club had agreed to do. The only thing was, sometimes the minutes seemed to ramble, and often people didn't do what they were supposed to do because the secretary had failed to make it clear specifically who had agreed to do what and when they had agreed to get it done. Often the president of the club ended up doing most of the work along with one or two others who could be counted on to follow through.

Eventually, I was elected president of that chapter of the AMA, and the notebook was handed over to me. I took the job because I liked the exposure, and it looked good on my resume. But I realized I was probably going to have to work like the dickens that year to get my paying job done as well as my new volunteer job. After all, I had no authority over any of the other officers or members even though I was now president. Every person in the group was a volunteer. Any one of them could walk at any moment, and any one could decide not to follow through on a commitment. I had no power over them, nor did I have recourse such as a performance review.

I Put This System In Place

The first thing I did was change the way the minutes were kept. At my ad agency we used action reports, which as you know are like minutes except they cut to the chase.

The Value of a Team Notebook

A notebook will:

• Give order to meetings

• Place focus on meeting objectives

• Outline procedures

• Provide consistency

• Serve as a history

• Be a public record

• Be an audit vehicle for the primary team

• Orient newcomers

• Allow others to pick up and carry on

They don't ramble on or recap a discussion, they report the decisions made and the actions to be taken. They clearly state who has responsibility for the action and the deadline agreed upon to get it done.

Second, I didn't just stick these action reports in the notebook to sit there until they were pulled out again and read at the next meeting, I sent a copy to all of the directors whether or not they'd been in attendance at the meeting, and I sent a copy to anyone else who might in any way be affected by the decisions which had been made.

I didn't stop there. Our chapter had a monthly newsletter and the president always wrote a column that appeared on the front page. I used that space to call attention to the people who had taken on different tasks, to give them a pat on the back for stepping up to the plate and committing to a specific date. I also praised those who had completed tasks already, or had made a special contribution.

And I didn't stop there. The president always opened the monthly luncheon meetings, so I used my time at the podium to say who was doing what and the deadline they were working toward. I'd ask them to stand to give them recognition. People like to hear their names and they like the spotlight. I'm sure the exposure made them feel warm all over because they, like me, had joined the organization in order to meet people, to network, and to become better known in the marketing community of our city.

Now let me ask you this. After all that exposure—once all their peers knew what they were supposed to accomplish—do you suppose any of those people dropped the ball? Of course not. If they had, whose reputation do you think would have suffered? Not mine—theirs. If they wanted business from other AMA members in a position to sent it their way, they'd have accomplished exactly the opposite. They'd have been viewed as individuals who don't follow through, individuals who let me and others down. So that year our AMA volunteers not only followed through, they followed through big time. More got accomplished in more spectacular ways than had been the case in even the longest-standing member's memory.

Use Awards to Motivate

The chapter gave an award each year called the Golden Candlestick to the person seen as having gone above and beyond and contributed more than anyone else. As the year unfolded, I often lamented from the podium that I didn't see how we were going to choose just one recipient because so many had contributed so much.

This brings up another point. Awards can be a great way to call attention to people and get them working enthusiastically. Bill Monahan in *Billion Dollar Turnaround* writes about one he created called the "Top Performer's Award." Rather than just give bonuses and recognition to the sales force, he expanded this practice to include the rest of the company. Each year his primary team would choose top performers who had gone above and beyond what was expected in their jobs to achieve outstanding results. Everyone at Imation had the opportunity to nominate whomever they felt was deserving. And rather than recognize only the winners, Bill also included spouses and partners, so the impact of what had been achieved would be felt within the family as well as by peers in the company. Recipients came from all different functions, all different levels, and from other countries as well as the United States. A daytime meeting would be held of the entire headquarters staff, where coffee and ice cream or cake would be served. Winners would be flown in from wherever they lived and worked. There'd be a guest speaker, and recipients would then receive their awards in front of this assembly. Announcements of the Top Performer Award winners were sent to hometown press and included in the company newsletter and on the web site. They included a photograph of each and rundown of accomplishments that had led to the award. This practice became so popular and generated such enthusiasm that business units in the different countries began having their own similar award programs in addition to the worldwide program.

Praise is More Powerful Than Money

I learned something valuable that year as president of the local chapter of the American Marketing Association. Praise is a powerful tool. It can be more powerful than money. Praise works because it makes people feel good, and people like to feel good. Money can't always buy that. And praise works for another reason. If everyone knows someone is supposed to complete a task—if all of their

peers know because you praised them for taking it on—
that person is almost surely going to do it, and do it well.

THAT YEAR, my term as AMA president whizzed by.
Things got done just the way they were supposed to. And
you know what? The Richmond Chapter won "Chapter of
the Year" out of more than a hundred or so contestants
across the United States and Canada.

It was the first time we had ever won, but it was not the
last time. And you know why? Because everyone involved
saw how to create a championship team. You can create
one, too. You can reach the high level of success you long
for and be the standout in your company or industry by
following the process described here. And best of all, you
won't even have to work as hard as you did before—back
when you were doing almost all of it yourself.

Stephen Hawley Martin is the co-author of *Lean Advertising,* author of half a dozen novels and non fiction books, and the editor of two best selling titles that have had a significant impact on the lean movement, *Lean Transformation* and *Product Development for the Lean Enterprise.* Now Publisher of The Oaklea Press, he is a former principal of The Martin Agency, a top-tier advertising and marketing communications firm serving such distinguished clients as UPS Package Delivery, GEICO Automobile Insurance, Vanilla Coke, and America Online.